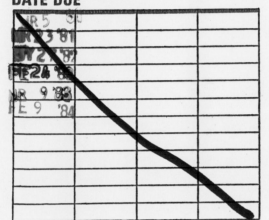

THE OFFENSIVE
AND DEFENSIVE

Coaching Line Game

Other Publications by the Author—

Championship Football Drills for Teaching Offensive and Defensive Fundamentals and Techniques

Quarterback Generalship and Strategy

The Complete Kicking Game: Mechanics and Strategy

30 Days to Go! A Pre-Season Football Conditioning Program

Rose Bowl Championship Football Offense, co-authored with Coach Jack Mollenkopf, Purdue University; 35 mm. filmstrips, with accompanying handbooks, 6 sets

Blueprinting Your Coaching Career

Coaching the Offensive and Defensive Line Game

by

Donald E. Fuoss

PARKER PUBLISHING COMPANY, INC.
WEST NYACK, NEW YORK

Dedication

to

Frances and Donna

What This Book Will Show You

The line game deals exclusively with the offensive and defensive line fundamentals, skills and techniques which are taught and utilized in present-day football. An effort has been made to compile and incorporate all of the up-to-date methods on the "how to" of line play. No other book deals with the subject as comprehensively as this one.

Good performance in football necessitates knowledge and execution of the two basic fundamentals, blocking and tackling. Therefore, if a coach will teach sound basic fundamentals and techniques, both offensively and defensively, he will produce a winner. However, he must first evaluate and slot his personnel properly, then organize them and teach the fundamentals, skills and techniques which are utilized in present-day football. Part I—COACHING AND PRACTICE SCHEDULE ORGANIZATION—consists of three chapters, offering aids and guides to help the football coach develop, evaluate and slot his personnel properly. Its purpose is to aid the coach in getting his players in positions where they can make the optimum contribution to the success of the team. Sample rating scales are included, showing the coach *what* to look for and *how* to compile valid and reliable information and data on each of his prospects. Sample forms are also included to illustrate how assignment and technique performance may be graded to determine the efficiency of the performer. The concluding chapter in Part I deals with a method of organizing the practice schedule in order to teach *A*gility, *B*locking and *C*ontact or tackling skills, the *A, B, C*'s of football.

Regardless of the offense which a coach employs, the most important ingredient for success is the proper execution of the fundamental blocks. Good, sound blocking is the heart and soul of offensive football. Part II—COACHING OFFENSIVE LINEMEN—consists of five chapters of *what, why* and *how* you teach offensive line fundamentals, skills and techniques, and *when* these should be utilized. The *who* to block will depend on each coach's system or the offensive plays

7

which he employs, although numerous diagrammatic illustrations are included which a coach may wish to adopt.

Coaching points are offered throughout the five chapters on offensive line play, commencing with the initial chapter wherein more than a dozen principles or "musts" for successful line blocking are explained and illustrated. All successful line blocking is predicated upon the application of this information. Other chapters deal with specific fundamentals, skills and techniques for individual positions, such as the center, interior linemen, tight ends and flankers. The concluding chapter in Part II deals with probably the most important aspect of offensive line play in present-day football—pass blocking fundamentals, skills and techniques.

Part III—COACHING DEFENSIVE LINEMEN/LINEBACKERS—consists of five chapters dealing with their fundamentals, skills and techniques. A separate chapter is included on pass rush principles and techniques, since this is a very important phase of the modern-day game. Defensive end and linebacker play are discussed in separate chapters, too.

Since tackling is the ultimate in defensive football, the concluding chapter in the book deals with the fundamentals and techniques of tackling. A good, hard-tackling team is hard to defeat, and probably the best barometer of a team's morale is its tackling effectiveness. Defensively, a team is no better than its tackling.

This book is intended for all football coaches, and prospective coaches, regardless of their level of competition or experience. *Coaching the Offensive and Defensive Line Game,* although written primarily for the coach or player as a specific reference book, may be used as a training manual or handbook for the physical education major, or the undergraduate and graduate student in the theory of coaching football course. All should find this book an invaluable source of information.

A recognized football axiom is, "Football games are won and lost in the line," because a corollary football axiom is, "A team cannot win if it cannot control the game on the line-of-scrimmage." This book is devoted entirely to line play—where games are won and lost. Since this is where the action is, this is what the book is all about—the offensive and defensive line play fundamentals, skills and techniques which are taught and utilized in present-day football.

Donald E. Fuoss

ACKNOWLEDGMENTS

Grateful appreciation is herewith expressed to all persons who shared in the preparation of this book. No claim of originality is made for much of the material contained in it. The interpretations and applications, however, are my responsibility.

I am grateful to Coach Milt Von Mann, Talent Scout, Kansas City Chiefs, for permitting me to quote and paraphrase parts of his material in order to make it applicable to the high school and college football coach.

Grateful appreciation is also expressed to Mr. Raymond Hunt for preparing the diagrams, to Mrs. Sarah Holloway, teacher and to her young ladies (seniors) of Vocational Office Education (clerical), Central High School, Murfreesboro, Tennessee, for typing the manuscript.

Finally, loving appreciation is expressed to my wife, Fran, our daughter, Donna and to my mother, for their assistance, encouragement, understanding and unfailing support.

D. E. F.

Contents

8. Coaching Offensive Line Passing Game Fundamentals, Skills and Techniques 138

PART III–COACHING DEFENSIVE
LINEMEN/LINEBACKERS

L E G E N D

○	Offensive Player
●	Ball Carrier
□	Center
⊘	Pulling Lineman (or Key Blocker)
Ⓧ	Split End
Ⓨ	Tight End
Ⓩ	Flanker Back
Ⓡ	Running Back
Ⓕ	Fullback
Ⓒ	Coach
■	Large Dummy

⟶ (hatched arrow)	Path of Ball Carrier
⟶ (dashed arrow)	Path of Player
⟶ (double-bar arrow)	Backfield Fake
⟶ (dotted arrow)	Forward Pass
⋁	Defensive Lineman
⊭	Defensive End
▽	Defensive Tackle
⩔	Noseman or Middle Guard
▷	B (W,M,S) Linebacker
W	S Secondary Defenders (Safeties)
C	H Defensive Cornerbacks/Halfbacks

I

COACHING AND PRACTICE SCHEDULE ORGANIZATION

Few football prospects want to be interior linemen because line play is hard work and little glory! While all prospects like to play a position that has a special attraction—such as handling the football, either passing or catching it or running with the ball—not all players have the skills or abilities to play such positions.

Backs and ends would rather play on offense than on defense because they can catch passes, run for touchdowns and get their names in the newspapers. The offensive backs and ends get more publicity throughout the season than the defensive ones, and they all get more recognition and credit than the linemen. During a game, every time an offensive back or end touches the football his name goes out over the loudspeakers and radio broadcasts. Therefore, it is a natural inclination for a football prospect to want to be an offensive back, preferably a quarterback or running back, or a receiver, preferably a wide flanker, since this is the glamor of football.

Control the Line-of-Scrimmage

Linemen, on the other hand, are required on almost every play to engage in close-in combat with the opposition. Even when a lineman carries out his assignment perfectly, seldom is he noticed by the spectator. Therefore, few prospects want to be interior linemen. Yet it is a recognized axiom, "Football games are

1

Line Play— Hard Work and Little Glory!

won and lost in the line," because a corollary football axiom is, "A team cannot win if it cannot control the game on the line-of-scrimmage."

OFFENSIVE LINE PLAY

Although football has improved in techniques and scope through the years, the basic precept that football games are won up front remains the same. A backfield of outstanding players has little chance to display its ability behind a poor blocking line. Without good blocking by the linemen, the backs would seldom get the necessary running room beyond the line-of-scrimmage. A ball carrier can usually go only as far as effective blocking takes him. If a team expects to win consistently, this must be well past the line-of-scrimmage into the defensive secondary. In football, the successful offense is one that is built around sound blocking techniques. Regardless of the offense a coach employs, the most important ingredient for success is the proper execution of the fundamental blocks.

Approximately 90 per cent of all offensive action or energy in football is used in blocking. Good blocking is the essence of good football. It is the distinguishing characteristic of a good offensive football team. Offensive football and the success of a well-designed offense is dependent upon sharp, crisp blocking by each and every member of the team. Good, sound blocking is the heart and soul of offensive football. Offensive line play personifies the true spirit of football. Chapters 4–8 will deal with coaching the fundamentals, skills and techniques of offensive line play.

DEFENSIVE LINE PLAY

The most important yard in any football game is the one which separates the offensive and defensive lines. The long passes and exciting runs that bring crowds to football games depend upon control of this yard. If the offensive line cannot dominate and control it, a non-existent, non-productive offensive attack is unlikely to produce many wins.

Conversely, if the defensive linemen cannot control the line-of-scrimmage, the offensive blockers will literally blow the defenders out of their positions, and the defensive backs will be weary from making numerous tackles and saves deep in their own secondary. However, interior linemen prefer defense to offense, as a defensive player can use his hands, play with reckless abandon and have "fun." If a defensive lineman does not have "fun," he probably does not like to play football. Defensive line play is hit or be hit, and you must hit to win. Most football prospects would rather hit than be hit, and if they do not play to win, then they are participating in the wrong sport!

Tackling is the ultimate in defensive football. A poor tackling team affects the morale and reduces the total effectiveness of its own offense by limiting its offensive scoring opportunities when it fails to force the opposition to give up the ball. On the other hand, a good, hard-tackling defensive football team usually is difficult to defeat, and limits the number of times the opposition has the football. Probably the best barometer of a team's morale is its tackling effectiveness. Defensively, a team is no better than its tackling. The highest tribute a team can be paid is to be called a fine, hard-tackling football team. Chapters 9–13 will deal with coaching the fundamentals, skills and techniques of defensive line play and linebacking.

COACHING LINE PLAY FUNDAMENTALS, SKILLS AND TECHNIQUES

Good performance in football necessitates knowledge and execution of the two basic fundamentals, blocking and tackling. The team which executes these two skills the best will be the winner. Therefore, if a coach will teach sound, basic fundamentals and techniques, both offensively and defensively, he will produce a winner. However, he must first evaluate and slot his personnel properly, and then organize his time and practice schedule in order to develop his personnel and teach the fundamentals, skills and techniques which are employed in present-day football. Chapters 2–3 deal with these aspects of coaching linemen.

Regardless of the level of competition, football coaches must be concerned with selecting personnel according to certain specifications. These will vary with the personnel available to the coach and the system of football employed.

Placing or Slotting Players Properly

The football coach who is the consistent winner is the one who successfully places or slots each individual player where he can use his potential to the utmost, and can make the maximum contribution to the success of the football team. While most experienced coaches have an insight or "knack" for recognizing and evaluating "talent," personal convictions and feelings are not sufficient, and are seldom valid and reliable as the sole means of evaluating and slotting personnel properly. Methods of securing factual information in order to evaluate linemen will be discussed in greater detail shortly.

Personnel Depends on System, and Vice Versa

The selection of personnel is also based on the type of offense and defense which a coach employs. As an illustration, if you favor primarily a power attack, then logically you should have big, strong linemen who can use their size to advantage. Conversely, if your available line personnel are physically small, then

2

Coaching Aids for the Selection of Line Personnel

you are not likely to be successful employing a power type of attack.

As a further illustration, if a coach employs a pulling type of offensive attack, or he likes to stunt on defense, then he would have to sacrifice size somewhat for agility and quickness in order to get his available personnel to execute these skills effectively on offense and/or defense. If the linemen are big, but not quick afoot, then a pulling attack is not likely to be successful. However, a straight-ahead power attack would permit these linemen to utilize their bulk and size advantageously.

Receivers, preferably tall and rangy with good speed, who can maneuver to get open and then make the reception, are essential if your offense is built around the passing game. If the receivers are short in stature, they may be able to catch the football, but if they are also slow afoot then the offense would be operating at a disadvantage if you try to exploit the passing game.

Therefore, the offense and defense a football team employs will be based on the personnel available to the coaching staff.

Look for *Athletes* First

Let us examine the criterion the professional football talent scouts employ in evaluating personnel. Since all things are relative at the respective levels of competition, the following information should prove helpful to *all* coaches.

Grateful appreciation is expressed to Coach Milt Von Mann, Talent Scout, Kansas City Chiefs, for permitting me to include much of his evaluation material here, and with his knowledge and permission, for permitting me to paraphrase some of it so it is applicable to high school and college football coaches. In talking with Coach Von Mann, he said, "I try to find the *athlete first,* and then fit him into the most desirable offensive or defensive position, instead of looking first for just a football player!" This is good advice for the high school and college football coach, too.

CHARACTERISTICS OF AN ATHLETE

The characteristics of a football prospect which should be measured or evaluated are as follows: speed, agility and balance, strength, toughness, desire, quickness and explosion, size potential, character, aggressiveness, pride and reaction time. Each will be discussed separately, although the presentation will be limited to offensive and defensive linemen and linebackers.

Speed

For the proper placement of his personnel, it is imperative a coach has *accurate* times for all of his players. A common mistake in evaluating players is merely to judge them in relation to the other squad members, and not time them accurately. After timing your players in sweats or shorts, and in full football gear, you will be able to place them in positions where they can utilize their speed to the best advantage for the team.

As a football coach, you should attempt to determine *football* speed, too, which is quickness in an immediate area. It is the speed or quickness a defensive lineman, as an illustration, moves from tackle to tackle, and *not* how fast he runs 50–100 yards. Movement in football refers to speed, quickness and agility. The latter two qualities are actually more important than speed, although lacking any of these three assets will limit the progress of a player. Therefore, except at a few positions in football, speed is *not* measured in "raw terms"; i.e., how fast a player can run 50–100 yards.

Agility and Balance

This characteristic or attribute is a combination of quickness and ease of movement which enables a player to be exceptional in balance and maneuverability. The development of body control, agility and the ability to react quickly and correctly are as important as the proper development of offensive and defensive fundamentals. Without the former required skills, a player will be unable to execute the necessary fundamentals. If a player is unable to control his own body, he will not be able to control his opponent.

As a coach, one can observe agility and balance in evaluating line personnel as follows:

1. Change of direction or position from coach's hand signal.
2. Sled drills, spin drills, hit and recovery drills, etc.
3. End's (back's) ability to change direction, cross over, etc.
4. Follow-through on 1-on-1 block.
5. Pass protection blocking, hit and recover.
6. End's ability to regain balance when held up or "bumped."
7. Balance in tackling and blocking drills.
8. End's (back's) ability to regain balance when hit.

Strength

Many football prospects with good physical size are not strong! In seeking the placement of linemen, the coach is looking for a prospect with the physical strength to defeat an opponent. The following are ways to observe strength:

1. Ball carrier's (receiver's) ability to run through tacklers and get extra yardage.
2. Pass blocker's ability to keep from being over-powered.
3. Defensive lineman's ability to over-power the blocker and get to the passer.
4. Defensive lineman's ability to defeat a double-team block.
5. Offensive lineman's ability to "drive out" a defensive man in a 1-on-1 situation.

Toughness

Coaches speak frequently of being "mentally" and physically tough, with the latter being more evident and easier to evaluate than the former. Taking into consideration the football season is long in duration, and the successful coach must build for the entire season and not just for a single game, the following observations may be made of your line prospects in order to determine their mental and physical toughness:

1. Is he susceptible to injury?
2. Does he recover quickly from injury?
3. Does his efficiency drop noticeably because of minor pain or bruises?
4. Does he need "prodding" by the coaching staff?

Desire

Great desire to excel on the part of a mediocre football prospect permits him to get the job done many times over the more skilled performer with less motivation or desire to excel. Coach Von Mann describes the characteristics of desire as follows:

1. The eagerness and persistency with which he attacks his job.
2. The intense desire to carry out an assignment successfully.
3. The relentless and emotional drive of a player when engaged in competition. His instinctive urge to dominate.

Quickness and Explosion

The ability of a player to move his feet, arms and body quickly is one of the characteristics of a good athlete. The following are ways to observe quickness and explosion:

1. Quick movement of the feet.
2. Rapid delivery of a blow.
3. Fast offensive and defensive start without command.
4. Quick movement in any direction.
5. The ability of a player to explode through an opponent and retain leverage, balance and follow-through.
6. The ability of a defensive lineman to explode into and neutralize the blocker, and yet maintain a good football position.
7. A tackler's ability to explode through a ball carrier.

Size Potential

Size potential means a player's capability of reaching the minimum height and weight requirements for his position in order to be an outstanding competitor in your league or calibre of competition.

The following suggestions are offered in making observations of size potential of prospects:

1. Is the player lean because of participation in another sport (wrestling)?
2. Has the prospect reached his maturity of growth? Some boys reach growth maturity at a very young age.
3. Does the prospect have a large-boned body structure?
4. Try to project the weight potential according to the requirements of the position; i.e., tackles are usually larger than guards, ends are generally leaner than tackles, etc.
5. How large are the prospect's parents?

Character

An *athlete* generally has outstanding "character," which is a combination of mental qualities in football, including the ability to inspire and lead others to perform more effectively. Some ways of observing this inherent quality are as follows:

1. He leads by example and not by talking.
2. Does he have the poise and confidence to calm down his team-mates under adverse conditions?
3. Do his teammates have utmost confidence in his ability to perform in a "clutch" situation?
4. Is he a good student?
5. Is he a leader, prominent in student government and other school activities?

Aggressiveness

Aggressiveness is the willingness and readiness to hit, and is a bold and energetic pursuit of a goal. The following are ways of observing aggressiveness in a prospect:

1. Pocket pass protection for linemen (and backs).
2. Full speed in head-on tackling.
3. Loves contact!
4. In the pass rush, is he rough on the blockers protecting the passer?

Pride

Pride is identifiable in a player when he displays a burning desire to win and the willingness to "pay the price" in hard work and sacrifice. Some ways of observing "pride" in an athlete are as follows:

1. Does he fight harder when the going gets rough?
2. Does he perform extra work to correct a weakness?
3. Does he offer excuses?

Pride and desire go together. They are almost inseparable. There is the desire to excel, the pride and satisfaction of getting the job done, whipping your man on either offense or defense, being a part of a winning football team, etc.

Reaction Time

This is a superior quality of instant counter-action to the movement of an opponent. Ways to observe reaction time are as follows:

1. A defensive lineman's ability to react to a trap block.
2. The ability of an offensive lineman to adjust his block to an opponent's moves.

3. A receiver's (or back's) ability to react and change his direction as a ball carrier or blocker, and the proper use of blockers.
4. The ability of a defensive player to recognize a fake quickly and pursue immediately and effectively.

Top Prospect—100% Athlete

Talent Scout Von Mann concludes this section of his "Characteristics of an Athlete" by stating, "A top prospect must be 100% athlete!"

SUGGESTIONS FOR SCOUTING POSITIONS IN FOOTBALL

The second section of Talent Scout Von Mann's brochure, "Suggestions for Scouting Positions in Football," is meaningful to high school and college coaches, too, who are seeking to a lesser degree the same type of personnel the professional football teams are looking for. Talent Scout Von Mann's final point for *all positions* is as follows: "Be able to discuss his ruggedness, durability and desire with the head football coach." While he is referring to the talent scout's discussion with the college coach, and in turn his own talks with the professional football coach and team for whom he is working in lining up talent, it is interesting to note that Coach Von Mann concludes each position by inquiring about two tangible characteristics, "ruggedness and durability," and one intangible, inherent quality, "desire." All three characteristics are "musts" at every level of competition in order to produce winners.

Offensive Linemen

In evaluating offensive line prospects, the following information is imperative:

1. Discuss speed thoroughly, supplementing this with comments on initial charge, ability, quickness, coordination and reaction qualities.
2. Evaluate blocking ability. Does he have a good initial charge? Is he a good position blocker?
3. Does he keep his feet and maintain contact?
4. Does he take pride in really driving an opponent out?
5. Evaluate his ability at close line blocking, trap blocking, downfield blocking and pass protection blocking.

6. Can he pull and lead interference and do a good job of blocking?
7. Has he been successful because of his size and strength?

Offensive Centers

In evaluating offensive centers, the following information is important:

1. Can he make the long snap to the punter both quickly and accurately? (If he is a good center prospect, but weak in making the long pass for the punt, a coach may use another prospect who does this well.)
2. Is he agile enough to pull out of the line and block a rushing linebacker or defensive end?
3. Does he have the same abilities as the other offensive linemen (described above)?

Flankers/Split Ends–Tight Ends

Flankers, split ends and tight ends may be evaluated as follows:

1. Analyze his type of speed. Has he the ability to "cut" sharply either way when running at full speed?
2. Does he depend on his speed or his faking ability to get into the open?
3. Does he run good patterns? Is his timing good?
4. Does he run hard and decoy well when he is not the intended receiver?
5. Does he have good, "sure" hands that can catch the ball "clean," or is he the bobbling catcher type?
6. Is he better at long or short patterns? Does he fight to get the football on all occasions?
7. When closely guarded, does he have the pronounced ability to come up with the "tough" catch?
8. Evaluate his ability to get away from an opponent who is trying to keep him from getting out for a pass.
9. Rate his ability as a ball carrier after he catches the pass.
10. Evaluate his blocking ability, both on the line and downfield.

Defensive Tackles (Interior Linemen)

The following information is pertinent to evaluating defensive tackles:

1. Evaluate his speed thoroughly, relevant to his initial charge, ability, quickness, coordination and reaction qualities.
2. Does he have a quick, fast charge?
3. Does he come on a tough charge and raise havoc?
4. Can he control his opponent and diagnose the play?
5. Evaluate his tackling ability.
6. Does he have good pursuit qualities?
7. Does he have strong arms and hands?
8. Evaluate his ability to handle running plays directly at him and to either side of his position.
9. How does he react to trap plays?
10. Has he been successful mainly because of his size and strength?

Linebackers

The following criteria may be used to evaluate linebackers:

1. Does he have the ability and "knack" to diagnose plays and react quickly?
2. Does he have the keen desire for contact?
3. Can and does he meet the play in the hole?
4. Evaluate his tackling ability thoroughly.
5. Can he effectively hold up the ends?
6. Evaluate his type of speed.
7. Does he have good pursuit qualities?
8. Can he cover the swing patterns quickly in flat territory and downfield?
9. Does he play outside or inside linebacker?
10. Can he play in the line on defense?
11. Does he call defensive signals?
12. Do you consider him strongest against running plays or pass defense?

Defensive Ends

The following information is relevant in evaluating defensive end personnel:

1. Evaluate his type of speed.
2. Rate him as rushing the passer.
3. How does he handle running plays to the inside and outside?

4. Evaluate his ability as a crasher, and also his techniques if called upon to cover the flat territory.

5. Is he a "smashing" tackler? Evaluate his roughness and agility.

6. Does he use his hands well against his blockers and control them or do the blockers get to his body easily?

7. Does he diagnose and react quickly?

8. Discuss fully with the head coach his ruggedness, durability and desire (which is the final point for *all* of the previously mentioned positions).

COMPOSITE GRADE FOR EACH ATHLETE-FOOTBALL PLAYER

The above-listed information indicates what to look for in evaluating an athlete-football player. Just as each talent scout evaluates each prospect, a coach at any level of competition can use a rating scale to evaluate his own prospects. Diagram 2-1 illustrates the characteristics described previously, which may be evaluated as follows: (1) *Outstanding;* (2) *Above Average;* (3) *Average;* (4) *Below Average;* (5) *Poor.*

Diagram 2-1

Rating scale for evaluating prospects.

Characteristics

	1	2	3	4	5	Rating Scale:
1. Speed						1. Outstanding
2. Agility						
3. Quickness						2. Above Average
4. Toughness						
5. Desire						3. Average
6. Strength						
7. Size Potential						4. Below Average
8. Coordination						
9. Aggressiveness						5. Poor
10. Pride						

Offensive Ability_____

Defensive Ability_____

Best Position and Why_____

If Player is a Reject, Indicate Why_____

Use the following rating scale guide-
```
   1.0 - 1.6 Star              2.9 - 3.4 Prospect
   1.7 - 2.2 Starter           3.5 - 4.0 Questionable
   2.3 - 2.8 Make the League    4.1      Reject
```

Rate prospect on offense_____; on defense_____.

Note in Diagram 2-1 that a Rating Scale *Guide* is also included in order to evaluate the prospect's potential, which is acquired by getting a sum of the ratings for the characteristics above and dividing by 10. If he is considered *a prospect;* i.e., rates no lower than 3.4 (composite grade), the appropriate form is completed (Diagrams 2-2 to 2-5), depending upon his particular offensive or defensive position. He is then rated as an offensive or defensive prospect, as indicated in Diagram 2-1.

METHODS OF EVALUATING PERSONNEL

The proper positioning of all the players will go a long way in assuring the success of your team. Such objective methods as film grading each player's performance in both practice and games and coaches' rating scales, along with the usual subjective methods that come mostly through experience, are invaluable means of determining personnel alignment. It is little wonder, then, that so much time is spent on evaluating personnel, and that alignment is usually the first item for discussion at every daily staff meeting during the season (and in spring practice).

Rating Scales

The following rating scales, supplied from the previously mentioned source of information, may be used by both the high school and college coach, as well as the professional football scout and coach, to evaluate player personnel. Rate each of the qualities for offensive and defensive linemen, and linebackers, as follows: (1) *Excellent;* (2) *Above Average;* (3) *Average;* (4) *Below Average;* (5) *Poor.*

Offensive Ends. A coach may rate his offensive ends as follows, as illustrated in Diagram 2-2.

Offensive Interior Linemen. A coach may rate his offensive interior linemen as follows, as illustrated in Diagram 2-3.

Defensive Linemen. A coach may rate his defensive linemen as follows, as illustrated in Diagram 2-4.

Linebackers. A coach may rate his linebackers as follows, as illustrated in Diagram 2-5 on page 40.

Evaluation—All Ways and Always

Evaluation is *all ways* and *always,* and in Chapter 3 methods of evaluating and grading a player's assignment and technique performance in practice and in game films will be presented. A coach's evaluation of a prospect should be based on as much valid and reliable *factual* information as he can secure on each prospective player.

Offensive Ends	1	2	3	4	5
Blocking:					
A-Straight Ahead					
B-Angle					
C-Double-Team					
D-Downfield					
Catching With Hands					
Faking					
Catching Ball in Crowd					
Running Ability After Catch					
Gets Open					
Adjustment of Speed for Catch					
Receiving Short					
Receiving Long					
Cutting Ability					
Strength					

Rating Scale:

1. Excellent

2. Above Average

3. Average

4. Below Average

5. Poor

Diagram 2-2

Rating scale for evaluating offensive end prospects.

Offensive Interior Linemen	1	2	3	4	5
Blocking:					
A-Straight Ahead					
B-Angle					
C-Trap					
D-Downfield					
E-Pulling Ability					
F-Drop Back Pass Protection					
G-Aggressive Pass Protection					
H-Roll-out Pass Protection					
Strength					

Rating Scale:

1. Excellent

2. Above Average

3. Average

4. Below Average

5. Poor

Diagram 2-3

Rating scale for evaluating offensive interior linemen.

Diagram 2-4

Rating scale for evaluating defensive line prospects.

Defensive Linemen	1	2	3	4	5
Ability to Defeat:					
A-Straight Ahead Block					
B-Angle Block					
C-Trap Block					
D-Double-Team Block					
Pass Rush					
Tackling					
Pursuit					
Strength					
Lateral Movement					

Rating Scale:

1. Outstanding

2. Above Average

3. Average

4. Below Average

5. Poor

Diagram 2-5

Rating scale for evaluating linebacker prospects.

Linebackers					
Ability Against Run:	1	2	3	4	5
A-Straight at Him					
B-Filling a Hole					
Pursuit					
Ability Against the Pass:	-	-	-	-	-
A-Pass Rush					
B-Pass Coverage					
Ability to Diagnose					
Wards-off Blockers					
Lateral Movement					
Tackling					
Strength					

Rating Scale:

1. Outstanding

2. Above Average

3. Average

4. Below Average

5. Poor

INTRODUCTION

Equally important as knowing *what* to look for in your line personnel (Chapter 2), is organizing a plan of *how* to develop and evaluate your linemen (Chapter 3).

By definition, *organization* is that "act or process of bringing together or arranging related parts into a whole." No phase of coaching is any more important than organizing your time and practice program so that all facets of the game receive adequate consideration and attention. The answer to successful coaching is good organization, regardless of one's coaching set-up. Although a coach must have good personnel and material plus good organization to win, he can have excellent material and lose if he is not a good organizer. Therefore, well-planned, detailed practice sessions are necessary. Since each coaching situation is different, the practice schedule and one's plan of organization must be "tailormade" to fit his particular situation. The following plan, adaptable to practically any coaching situation, is one which is suggested for teaching the A,B,C's of football to your offensive and defensive linemen and evaluating your line personnel.

THE A,B,C's OF FOOTBALL FOR LINEMEN

Somewhere in a football coach's daily practice plans he should incorporate *A*–Agility, *B*–Blocking and *C*–Contact or tackling drills, in or-

3

Coaching and Practice Schedule Organization for Developing and Evaluating Linemen

der to teach and develop these necessary game fundamentals, techniques and skills.

Four-Station Drills for Linemen

One method of organizing a 15-minute segment of the practice schedule in order to assess the agility reactions of *all* linemen, and teach and evaluate certain basic fundamental game skills and techniques, is the Four-Station Drills for linemen.

During spring practice, and in pre-season practice in the fall until prior to the first regular-season game, these drills may be used daily except on the days scrimmage is scheduled. During the regular season, the drills may be used on Monday and Tuesday of each week during September and into October. Later some of the "hitting" drills may be eliminated, but it is suggested that the players continue to do the warm-up, agility-reaction and form tackling drills, along with selected sled drills, throughout the entire football season.

Purpose and Value of the Drills. While the Four-Station Drills may also be used as a conditioner, their value lies in teaching and evaluating agility-reaction and specific basic skills of a segment of the game for the line personnel. It should also be kept in mind that while the linemen and line coaches are at one end of the field going through agility-reactions and the Four-Station Drills for 15 minutes, the flanker and backfield coaches are at the opposite end of the field running their personnel through a series of drills with similar objectives in mind. However, the presentation here will be limited in scope to the drills for linemen.

Warm-Up Drills or Exercises*

Prior to dividing the linemen into four groups, all players should go through a 5-minute, organized warm-up routine, in order to stretch and loosen the muscles in preparing for the more strenuous activity which will follow the warm-up period. It makes little difference whether it is the "quick-quick" routine or the more conventional stretching exercises. The entire sequence should be done rapidly in

---

* Donald E. Fuoss, *Championship Football Drills for Teaching Offensive and Defensive Fundamentals and Techniques* (Englewood Cliffs, N.J.: Prentice-Hall, Inc., 1964), pp. 313-321.

order to complete the warm-up routine in the 5-minute allotted time.

By following the same warm-up routine each day, the players soon become familiar with progression so that after several days it is not necessary to announce or explain the next exercise in the progression. The "leader" merely begins the next exercise, after a couple of hand claps, and the squad members follow, generally "talking it up" while doing the exercises (which should be encouraged). (*See* footnote source for 25 warm-up drills or exercises, half of which may be selected as a suitable warm-up routine.)

Organizing the Four Stations

On the sound of the horn, which indicates the squad will divide into designated groups, the linemen sprint to designated areas where the Four-Station Drills will be conducted, *after* 3 minutes of four agility-reaction drills, as indicated in Diagram 3-1. (Some coaches may prefer to do the warm-up exercises in these small groups at the various stations, although there is value in having the entire squad together initially in one large group before breaking up into small groups.)

Merely for the sake of organization and in order to divide the linemen (only) into small groups, on the sound of the horn these players go to designated areas with the following coach, who will be conducting *first* the agility-reactions, then a specific drill:

Station #1—Centers and linebackers to center-linebacker coach.

Station #2—Guards to the defensive line coach.

Station #3—Tackles to the offensive line coach.

Station #4—Ends (not flankers) to the defensive end coach.

If the coaching staff has only two line coaches, the above plan could still be employed by combining line personnel for Stations #1–2 with the defensive line coach, and the offensive line coach handling personnel for Stations #3–4. The personnel would then merely rotate back and forth between the two line coaches, with each coach conducting two drills each.

Nor is it necessary to have four stations, as this depends on the personnel and the number of coaches which are available. Obviously, the larger the coaching staff the more stations one could have. Nor is

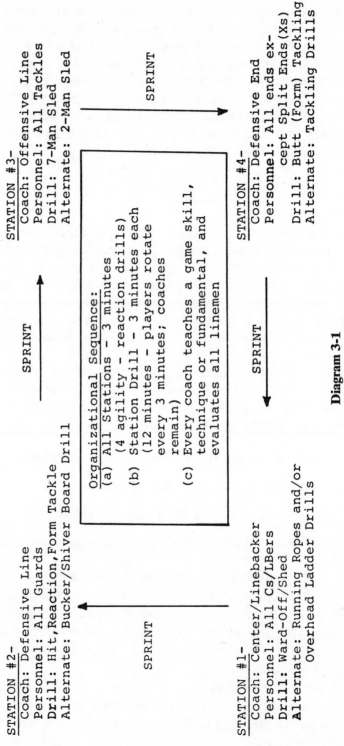

Diagram 3-1
Organizing the four stations.

it necessary to allot 3 minutes to the agility-reaction drills or a total of 12 minutes to the players rotating through the four stations. If the groups are relatively small in number (8–15), and each coach is *pushing* the participants as they execute the particular skill or technique at his station, 3 minutes will be of sufficient duration. A shorter period of time, when working with 8–15 prospects, is not adequate, and a longer period would be too demanding—if the drills are done properly.

Let us now look at the A,B,C's of football and see what should be taught or practiced daily.

A–Agility-Reaction Drills for Linemen

Select approximately four agility-reaction drills for a period of 3 minutes, which *all linemen* will perform at *all four* designated *stations* (before going into the specific skill or technique drills). There are any number of worthwhile and beneficial agility-reaction drills, such as: (1) Somersault or Forward Rolls Drill; (2) Carioca or Grapevine Drill; (3) Hip Opener Drill; (4) Lateral Wave Drill.** After the routine is established, one new drill may be added each week. (*See* footnote source for 37 football drills for teaching agility and reaction.)

Selection of Drills. There are many other worthwhile agility-reaction drills, but the objective is not variety or numbers. Part of the value of doing the same drills is familiarity, which leads to proficiency in performing the drill and mastering the skill, technique or fundamental involved.

Reaction drills may be utilized to develop both agility and reaction; whereas, simple agility drills are limited in value unless a stimulus (sight or sound) is added, along with the teaching of mobility and nimbleness, in order to secure the desired reaction. Therefore, as a coaching point, you should seldom employ drills that teach *only* agility, unless that particular agility is also a technique or fundamental of football.

Drill Guides and Suggestions.*** In getting the most out of the personnel and the drills—i.e., realizing the objective or purpose of the drill—the emphasis should be on *correct performance*. For this reason, in a number of the drills it is suggested they be set up in three-

---

** *Ibid.,* pp. 30-44.
*** *Ibid.,* pp. 8-13.

man units, which of course will depend on the number of players and coaches involved in the drills. As an illustration, in Diagram 3-2 each coach can handle 12 players without any difficulty by arranging four three-man units around his position. After working with a single unit (to his front), all the coach need do is turn quickly in a clockwise motion to the next three-man unit and repeat the procedure until all four units have been drilled. Therefore, it is possible for all players at each station to do all four of the selected agility-reaction drills in the 3 minutes of allotted time. (*See* footnote source for 23 drill guides and suggestions.)

Diagram 3-2
Organizing the agility-reaction drills in order to develop and evaluate personnel.

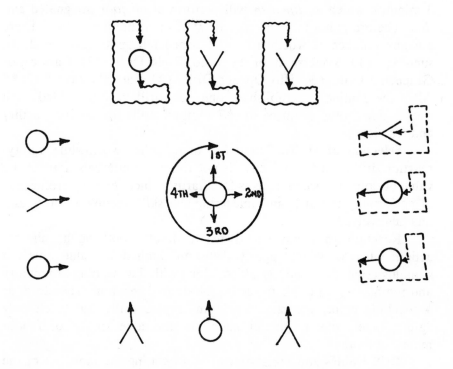

The Whistle Sounds. At the end of 3 minutes' duration, the whistle will be blown by a manager who is keeping time and the linemen now execute the *B's* and *C's* of football. However, the players remain at the *same stations*—do not rotate on the first whistle—to execute the drill which is designated for that particular station.

At the termination of 3 minutes the manager will blow the whistle again, and the players will sprint to the next station for 3 minutes of new drills.

The stations are 15–25 yards apart, depending on the amount of space needed to conduct the drill, but they are set up in clockwise fashion (Diagram 3-1), and at the end of 3 minutes (when the whistle sounds), the players sprint from one station to the next. Each coach remains at his respective station, and during a 3-minute period he can observe each player in his group. At the end of 3 minutes, the four groups of linemen all change. During a 12-minute period, each coach is able to observe and evaluate all of the linemen in the particular drill which he is conducting. Allowing 3 minutes for agility-reaction drills, at the end of 15 minutes this phase of teaching and evaluation is complete, and upon the sound of the manager's horn, the players and coaches are divided into groups to practice another phase of the organized program dealing with individual offensive and/or defensive techniques.

B–Blocking and C–Contact or Tackling Drills for Linemen

Through the organizational plan of four stations, the B's and C's of football are taught as follows, with *only* the purpose of the drill being included here. (*See* footnote reference for Procedure and Coaching Points, with page numbers listed in parentheses after each drill.)†

Station #1—Ward-Off and Shed Drill:† (pp. 232-233, 259).

Purpose: To develop use of flipper (or hands), warding off, shedding blockers, maintaining leverage and sustaining proper pursuit (Diagram 3-3).

Station #1A—Running Ropes and/or Overhead Ladder Drill:† (p. 43). (Although Station #1 drill is excellent, physically it takes a great deal out of the players. Therefore, if a coach intends to do rough work or scrimmage later in his practice session, it might be desirable to substitute another drill, such as utilizing running ropes and/or the overhead ladder if such facilities are available.)

Purpose: Ropes—to develop agility, body balance and coordination; *ladder*—to strengthen the shoulder muscles, thus reducing the frequency of shoulder dislocations, and as a conditioner.

---

† Donald E. Fuoss, *Championship Football Drills for Teaching Offensive and Defensive Fundamentals and Techniques* (Englewood Cliffs, N.J.: Prentice-Hall, Inc., 1964).

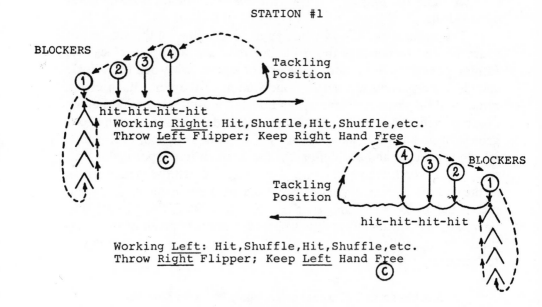

Diagram 3-3
Ward-off and shed drill.

Station #2—Hit, Reaction, Form Tackle Drill:†† (pp. 221-225).

Purpose: To teach and develop delivering a blow, reaction to (sight) movement, pursuit and form tackling (Diagram 3-4).

Station #2A—Bucker or Shiver Board Drill:†† (p. 235).
(Since form tackling is taught and practiced at Station #4, the bucker or shiver board drill may be substituted here at Station #2 if such equipment is available.)

Purpose: To teach and develop how to hand shiver properly, ward off and move the feet (Diagram 3-5).

Station #3—Sled Drill:†† (pp. 69-71, 84-85).

Purpose: Seven-man sled—to develop team starts and take-offs; two-man sled—to develop shoulder blocking techniques and control a moving object. *Note:* It is probably most expedient to utilize the seven-man sled for this drill since only 3 minutes are allotted in the practice schedule. However, some coaches set aside 5 minutes daily in their practice schedule (aside from this particular 15-minute seg-

†† *Ibid.*

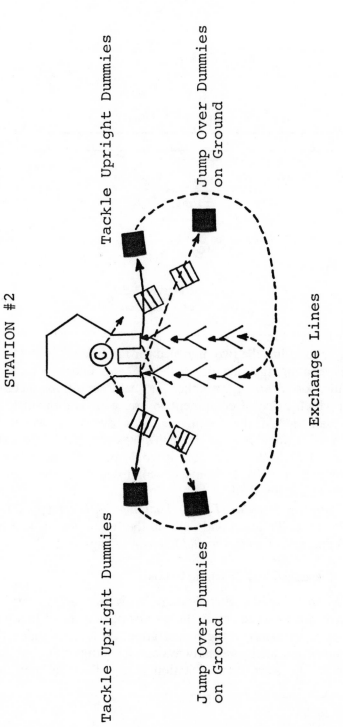

STATION #2

Tackle Upright Dummies

Jump Over Dummies
on Ground

Tackle Upright Dummies

Jump Over Dummies
on Ground

Exchange Lines

Diagram 3-4
Hit, reaction and form tackle drill.

STATION #2A

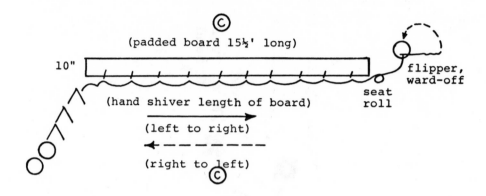

Diagram 3-5
Bucker or shiver board drill.

ment) for working on team starts and take-offs. In this case, it would be better to utilize the two-man sled for the Four-Station Drill, thereby not duplicating the take-off drill here and later on in the practice schedule, too. Secondly, weather and field conditions dictate to some extent which piece of equipment to use, as it is difficult to move the seven-man sled if the footing is poor due to inclement weather. Thirdly, if it appears your linemen's legs are getting "heavy" due to tiredness, length of season, etc., it would probably be better to substitute the two-man sled for the seven-man sled drill. However, it should be an offensive line drill.

Station #4—Butt (Form) Tackling Drill:††† (pp. 273-374).

Purpose: To teach and develop the fundamentals and techniques of tackling or C–Contact for *all* linemen (Diagram 3-6).

Organizational Coaching Points

When using the Four-Station Drills regularly, every couple of days it is advisable to rotate the groups of players so that each group is *not* always starting at the same station. As an illustration, instead of the centers and linebackers always commencing at Station #1, after a couple of days start them at Station #2, and several days later rotate

---

††† *Ibid.*

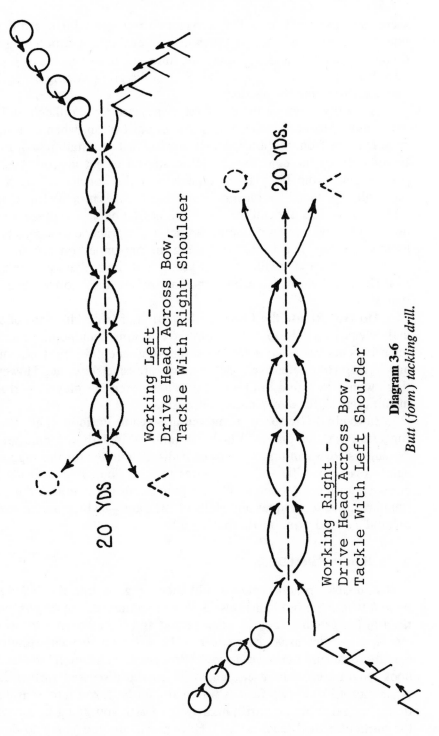

STATION #4

20 YDS

Working Left –
Drive Head Across Bow,
Tackle With <u>Right</u> Shoulder

Working Right –
Drive Head Across Bow,
Tackle With <u>Left</u> Shoulder

20 YDS.

Diagram 3-6
Butt (form) tackling drill.

them to Station #3, etc. This serves two purposes. First, a different line coach will have the opportunity to evaluate a different group doing the agilities at his station. In time, all four coaches will then have the opportunity to observe all four of the groups doing the agility-reaction drills, and by positions.

Secondly, some of the drills (stations) are more difficult and demand more physically than others. As an illustration, when a group of players move from Station #3 (seven-man sled) to Station #4, it will be difficult for the coach at the latter station to get a good, hustling performance from his players, especially if the coach at Station #3 has really "pushed" his players in moving the seven-man sled. Consequently, it will be difficult for the coach at Station #4 to make a valid and reliable evaluation of the personnel if the practice sequence is the same every day. However, by rotating the personnel, on occasion the coach at Station #4 will get each group first, immediately after agilities. He can then evaluate his personnel before they go to the seven-man sled.

Do Not Rotate the Coaches. If your staff is divided into offense and defense, there is no value, from the coaching standpoint, in having offensive coaches *teach* defensive skills, fundamentals and techniques, and having your defensive coaches *teach* offensive skills, etc. However, there would be value in different coaches *observing* players performing different skills for evaluation purposes.

Individual-Group or Combination-Team Periods. The above-suggested practice plan will take 20 minutes, including 5 minutes for the suggested warm-up exercises or drills, 3 minutes for the suggested agility-reaction drills and 12 minutes for the Four-Station Drills. By employing such a systematic plan, a coach does not overlook the basic fundamentals, techniques and skills of the game—which are necessary to build a sound, winning football team!

How to Select Drills

A coach's practice plan would then progress into the *individual period,* where the fundamentals, skills and techniques are *taught; practiced* in the *group* or *combination period* and then woven into overall offensive and defensive *team effort,* to be tested under game-simulated conditions during the *team period.* "Practice Organization" merits full book-length treatment itself, and will not be discussed further here other than to state two factors which should be taken into consideration when selecting any drill; namely: (1) Are you going to use what the particular drill teaches? (2) How much are you going to derive from the particular drill which you select? The *purpose* or *objective* of the drill will help you answer these questions. (*See* footnote source for a discussion on practice drill organization and administration.) §

EVALUATING AND GRADING PERFORMANCE

A coach should utilize both game and practice films to grade and evaluate the efficiency of his offense and defense, and his personnel. He can then determine accurately whether or not a player is getting the job done in terms of carrying out his assignment, and evaluate the player's (correct or incorrect) techniques. The coach can also determine whether or not he is playing his best personnel, and whether they are slotted properly. A coach can also determine what must be taught, practiced and coached during the week prior to the next game.

Grading Assignment Performance

For illustrative purposes *only* offensive assignment and technique performance will be included here, although the grading methods are applicable to defensive linemen, too. When a coach grades his offensive players, it is advisable to have the blocking categories broken down as follows:

GM (*Got Man*)—means the offensive blocker eliminates his man from the play, in that he does not give the defender an opportunity to make the tackle; i.e., *regardless of the technique employed* (correct or incorrect), the blocker knocks down his man, ties him up, walls him off, forces the defender to go behind (chase), etc., not giving the defender a chance to get in on the tackle.

MM (*Missed Man*)—means the offensive blocker goes after the proper defender; i.e., applies his blocking rule correctly, but *regardless of his technique* (correct or incorrect), he is unsuccessful in eliminating the defender from the play, in that the opponent has the opportunity to make the tackle.

MA (*Missed Assignment*)—indicates a *mental mistake* where the blocker either applies his blocking rule incorrectly (goes after the wrong defender) or does not attempt to block anyone.

If an offensive player continues to bust assignments he simply cannot play for you, despite the fact he is a good blocker when he goes

---

§ *Ibid.*, pp. 3-21.

after the proper defender. In the final analysis *MA* will hurt the offense more than *MM,* although both count a zero (0) in figuring blocking efficiency. The reasoning is not illogical. The busted assignment "frees" a defender who can make the big defensive play, which usually stops an offensive drive. When this occurs, there is also a good possibility of a fumble, an offensive turn-over and/or an injury to the quarterback or ball carrier. Usually the defender, many times a linebacker, comes through free with force and momentum and smashes into the offensive back before he gets possession of the football. The latter has little or no opportunity to protect himself, since the defender's sudden presence in the offensive backfield is totally unexpected.

Diagram 3-7 illustrates a sample work sheet which may be utilized to grade the efficiency of an individual lineman (offensive center). Note how the player's blocking efficiency drops off when he is graded down for *MA.* Grading techniques, illustrated in the right-hand column, will now be discussed.

Grading Technique Performance

The *technique* should *not* be figured in with, or have a bearing on, the totals when determining blocking efficiency, although some coaches feel otherwise. In the right-hand column (A) of Diagram 3-7, space is provided to note comments relevant to a player's technique. If he employs wrong techniques, then this should be called to his attention when he and his coach view the films together. In the practice sessions, the blocker should be coached and drilled to utilize the correct and proper techniques. In the final analysis, on every play an offensive player will either *GM, MM* or *MA,* regardless of the technique he employs. It is more important to be graded *GM,* even if a player uses the wrong techniques, than it is to be graded *MM* and the blocker adheres to all the correct techniques *except* he fails to eliminate the defender from the play. To grade a player unfavorably when he happens to *GM,* except he uses the *wrong* techniques, and to grade him favorably when he happens to *MM,* but uses the *correct* techniques, is an injustice to the player and is a fallacy in the grading system. The latter is merely a means to an end, and no grading system is the end in itself. Its purpose, in this instance, is to aid both the individual performer and the team, and is a means of evaluation for the coaching staff to do a better teaching job. Diagram 3-7 (A) illustrates one method of grading a player's technique performance. Another relatively simple

Player: __D.SMITH__   Position: ___CENTER___   Opponent: ___STATE___   (10 - 6)

Play	Def.	Opport.	GM	MM	MA	(A) Comments	(B) TECHNIQUES Approach	Contact	Follow-Through
24Pr.	O5-2			1		Not set;poor exchange-fumble;dipped your tail.	1	1	1
23Pr.	O5-2			1		Head behind M; he got T#1.	3	2	3
82	P4-3	No	-	-	-	No play; def.T o-s/pen.			
30Tr.	P4-3				1	Re-check your rule; block back, not 0; see me.			
Punt	odd	*	-	-	-	Low pass;punter hurried. Relax!Pass ball when ready.			
22Ts.	P4-3		1			Poor cut-off; M fell.			
G22Ts	4-4				1	B.S.P.,not ILB; re-check your rule; see me.			
37Dr.	G6-5	No	-	-	-	No; hard pinch on you.			
38L	G6-5		1			Exc.block on MLB. Techs. excellent,too!			
TOTS.	---	70	40	20	10	57% block.effic.can't win; let's work to improve!			

(Numbers indicate errors-techniques)

Approach:
1. Movement,i.e.,failure to get off with ball or starting **count**.
2. Improper angle or path of blocker.
3. Feet,i.e.,stepping with wrong foot first;steps too long,etc.

Contact:
1. Poor initial contact,i.e.,no "pop," too soft, etc.
2. Wrong shoulder;wrong technique.
3. Poor body position,i.e.,back bowed,head down,etc.

Follow-Through:
1. Failure to move feet.
2. Failure to sustain drive.
3. Falling to ground;feet in hole; other mistakes.

GM/Total Plays (exc.MA)=40/60=67% (but not true %).
GM/Total Plays (inc.MA)=40/70=57% blocking efficiency.
*Punts not figured with totals(merely correct errors)

Diagram 3-7

Forms for grading assignment and techniques performance.

method (not illustrated) is to mark a horizontal line (—) if the player satisfactorily performs all of the following: huddle break, hustles to the line-of-scrimmage, stance, alignment, takeoff and approach to the block. A vertical line (|) is awarded if the player gets his man. Thus, if the blocker performs all phases correctly, he has a horizontal line with a vertical line through it, forming a plus (+). If his performance is very poor, he receives a zero (0).

Therefore, 1 point is awarded for every vertical line (|); 1 point for every horizontal line (—); 2 points for every plus (+) mark and zero points for every zero (0). By multiplying the number of times technique and execution were properly performed (possible 2 points; i.e., a (+) for every play) by each of the above point ratings, you arrive at the total number of points graded. The total number of plays the player performed in the game is then multiplied by 2 and divided into the total number of points scored to get the efficiency percentage.

Technique Factors and Rating Scale. In Diagram 3-7 (B) in place of "Comments" on the right-hand side, the following three areas may be indicated and analyzed: *Approach, Contact, Follow-Through*. The numbers 1, 2 and/or 3 are then recorded by the coach in each of the columns to indicate the offensive lineman performed the technique or execution *incorrectly*. (The spaces are left blank when the player performs the technique correctly.) The left-hand side of Diagram 3-7 remains the same, and the player's efficiency grade as a blocker is determined in the same way as explained previously. The list in Diagram 3-7 (B) is by no means all inclusive. Other appropriate items could be listed under *Approach, Contact* and *Follow-Through* in evaluating performance of techniques.

There are other methods of grading offensive performance, where the grading system goes from 0–5, with 0 being awarded for the missed assignment and 5 being given for the excellent assignment, with most of the scores falling in the 1–4 category. The scores are averaged, and each player is given a numerical rating as well as a percentage rating. The offensive team must collectively average 3.0 or higher and 70 per cent or better on blocking assignments to show a potential winning performance.

Self-Evaluation

Since coaching is a race against time, a coach may employ player or self-evaluation methods where each player grades himself. In many cases, the player will prove to be more critical of himself than his coach. The main objective is to let the players see their mistakes, make them understand *why* they made those mistakes and develop a workable plan for eliminating errors and improving their play.

An arbitrary rating scale must be set up for grading so that the percentage figure has meaning and can be interpreted. Most coaches feel an individual rating of more than 80 per cent is excellent, and might be classified as championship performance, whereas anything below 59 per cent is a poor performance; 60–69 per cent is considered fair and usually 70–79 per cent is a winning performance.

Generally a team must grade better than 70 per cent in order to win, although they may grade lower or higher and win or lose, respectively, depending on how well their opponents played. Any objective, valid, reliable means may be employed to evaluate your personnel and their game performance. Any grading system is merely a means to an end, and is not the end in itself.

II

COACHING OFFENSIVE LINEMEN

Other things being equal, proficiency in fundamentals is the winning edge in athletics. Winning teams are made up of players who are well versed in the fundamental skills, which are developed through constant repetitive practice and coaching. Doing something *almost* right and doing it *exactly* right is usually the difference between failure and success. This statement could never be more true than when it is related to teaching and learning the fundamentals and techniques of offensive line play. Therefore, in this chapter let us consider certain basic fundamentals which *all* linemen must adhere to in order to block successfully, and coaching points or suggestions for teaching offensive line fundamentals, skills and techniques. Chapters 5–8 will be a discussion of offensive line techniques, and it will not be necessary there to reiterate any of the points made in this chapter.

THE PRINCIPLES OR "MUSTS" FOR SUCCESSFUL LINE BLOCKING

Regardless of the offensive line position or type of stance employed, there are certain basic principles *all* offensive linemen must be coached to adhere to *every* time in order to block successfully. If a player violates any of these basic principles, the chance of his offen-

4

Coaching Points for Teaching Offensive Line Fundamentals, Skills and Techniques

sive blocking being successful is definitely minimized.

Know the Offensive Play

The offensive team has two advantages over the defensive team: (1) they know the offensive play or the critical point-of-attack; (2) they know the offensive starting count. The failure of an offensive player to utilize fully either of these two advantages to the utmost is to minimize and drastically reduce the effectiveness of the offensive attack.

What Does "Knowing" the Offensive Play Mean? It means *not* leaving the offensive huddle without being *positive* of the play called by the quarterback.

Linemen do not concern themselves too much with offensive formations, unless they are flopping strong- and weak-side. If only the specialists flop, then the five interior linemen are even less concerned since their offensive positions never change. Nor are interior linemen concerned with offensive backfield sets, unless they receive assistance from a back in carrying out their particular offensive assignment. However, linemen should have some conception of the construction or design of the play. Is it a delayed play, power off-tackle or a quick hitter? Is it a straight drop-back pass, play action pass, semi-sprint pass or option run-pass? Offensive linemen should also know which is the *on*-side and the *off*-side of the play on every play, in order to block effectively. If it is a pass, knowing from where the pass will be thrown is vitally important in order to give proper protection to the passer. Diagram 4-1 illustrates a number of these important points.

Diagram 4-1 also illustrates how a single word, such as "Lee," "Blast," "Trap" or "Bootleg," changes the blocking scheme of play "28." Therefore, if the right guard, as an illustration, leaves the huddle hearing only "28," and he figures he should block "1" (as in 28 Lee), he would be correct in "knowing" the play or *who* to block only once out of the four plays illustrated.

Incidentally, to facilitate the learning of offensive blocking assignments, linemen should be taught to group plays with *similarity of assignments,* such as the drives, bucks, bellys, picks, etc., which are all quick-hitting plays with man-on-man blocking, and the five interior linemen merely block their respective number regardless of whether the plays go front- or back-side. (*See* Diagram 4-6 for numbering.)

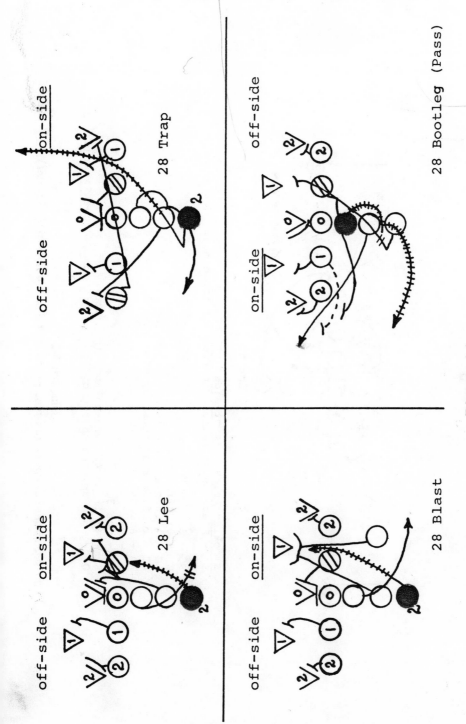

Diagram 4-1

Word after number changes design of play and blocking (28 lee, 28 blast, 28 trap, 28 bootleg pass).

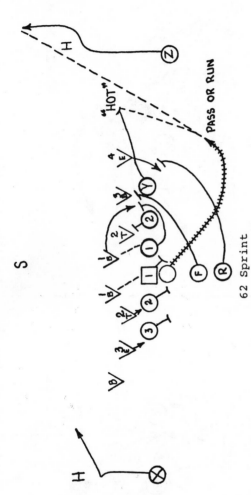

62 Sprint

Blocking Rules – Front-side Sprint:
Y – Flat; never release in front of force man; "Hot" vs.4-4.
RT – 2.
RG – 1.
C – 0; off-side.
LG – 1 if over or outside; otherwise 2.
LT – 2 if over or outside; otherwise 3.
X – Across.
Z – Up.
F – Cut 3.
R – 4; if no 4 clean-up on 3 (pursuit).
Q – Open up, get on hip of R; hit Y if open, otherwise run.

Diagram 4-2

Front-side sprint-out option run-pass versus split 6 or 4-4 defense (62 sprint).

Know the Offensive Starting Count

Defensive football is *reaction* football; *offensive* football is *assignment* football first, and then it is reaction to the defender's charge or his reaction to the play or the football. Since the defender will react immediately, the offensive blocker must get off with the starting count. If he fails to do so, the blocker sacrifices one of the two advantages which the offensive team has over the defensive team. Consequently, when a player breaks the huddle, it is imperative that he knows the offensive play and the starting count.

Know Your Assignment or *Who* to Block

A player generally "busts" his offensive blocking assignment because he does not know how to apply his blocking rules properly. This means in order to eliminate such faulty play, a coach should devise *simple* blocking rules, such as those illustrated in Diagrams 4-2 and 4-3. Then it is a matter of teaching, practice and application of blocking rules versus the various sets, until familiarity prevails. (*See* Diagram 4-6 A–N for identifying various defensive alignments and numbering defensive players.)

Diagram 4-2 illustrates the sprint-out option run-pass to the front or strong (Y's) side, and Diagram 4-3, to the weak (X's) side of the line, versus the Split 6 or 4-4 defense.

Know Offensive Line Splits and Defensive Spacing

All linemen are permitted to adjust their offensive line splits as they come to the line of scrimmage or *before* they go down into their set position. (Offensive ends are permitted to adjust *after* they have assumed their down stance.) Unless this is taught, coached and practiced, offensive linemen will inevitably take the same splits on almost every play.

Merely as a *point of reference,* Diagram 4-4 illustrates *basic, wide* and *tight* splits or spacing for offensive linemen. Certain offensive plays are better run from wide spacing, as an illustration, if defenders will permit the offense to take wider splits. Conversely, certain defensive alignments, such as a gap goal line defense, forces the offensive linemen to tighten their splits. The tactical situation has a direct bearing on both the offensive spacing and play, and, conversely, on the defensive alignment and spacing.

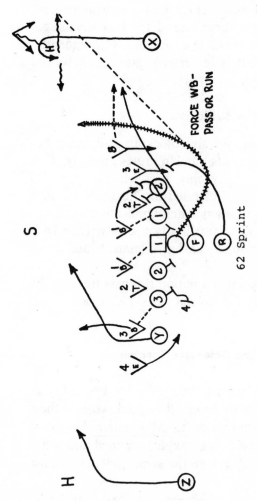

62 Sprint

Blocking Rules - Back-side Sprint:
Y - Across, beat far linebacker.
RT - 2.
RG - 1.
C - 0; off-side.
LG - 1 if over or outside; otherwise 2.
LT - 2 if over or outside; otherwise 3.
X - Up, if there; or hook and slide.
Z - Across.
F - Run at 3, continue to flat.
R - Cut 3.
Q - Open up, get on hip of R; hit FB
    in flat if open; otherwise X.

Diagram 4-3

Back-side sprint-out option run-pass versus split 6 or 4-4 defense (62 sprint).

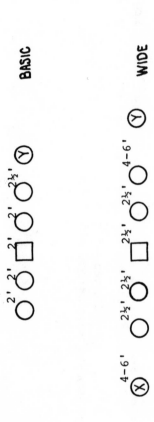

BASIC

WIDE

TIGHT

(Tighten to 6"between men)

Diagram 4-4

Suggested splits or spacing (and guides) for offensive linemen.

Guides for Offensive Line Splits – To aid an offensive lineman in adjusting his spacing properly, the following guides are offered:

1. Never split to a distance where a defender can beat you through the inside gap.
2. Take any spacing which will aid you in carrying out your assignment.
3. If the defender is inside of your position, move in.
4. If the defender is nose-on or over, adjust to help your blocking assignment.
5. If the defender is outside your position, move out.
6. No defender in your immediate area, adjust to aid your assignment or application of rule.

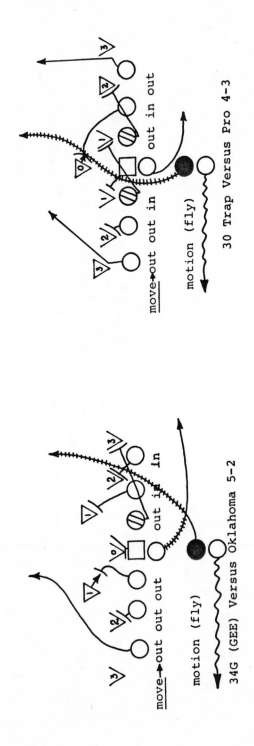

Diagram 4-5

Application of offensive line split guides (34 gee, 30 trap).

Diagram 4-4 also includes guides for offensive splits, which will aid an offensive lineman in adjusting his spacing properly.

Diagram 4-5 illustrates the application of these suggested guides —the fullback running off-tackle versus the Oklahoma 5-2 defense (left illustration) and the fullback trap versus the 4-3 defense (right illustration).

Defensive Spacing. Knowing defensive alignments and defensive spacing is important, too. In Diagram 4-5, in the Oklahoma 5-2 (left illustration), the defenders opposite the guards, tackles and ends are off-set on the outside shoulder of their respective counterpart. The defenders have split rules, too, and they will only off-set to the outside up to a certain point. If the offensive guards take wide spacing, the linebackers will either move up and shoot the gaps or one linebacker will move his middle guard into the wide seam and stack behind him. The middle guard will then shoot the gap.

By taking wide splits, the offensive guards and tackles will force their defenders to react by moving nose-up. If they take wider than normal splits, the defensive tackles and ends will move to the inside away from their blockers and shoot the seams.

Versus the 4-3 or the Pro 4-3 (Diagram 4-5, right illustration), if the offensive guards take wider than normal splits, the defenders (tackles) over them will move in and shoot the gaps. The offensive right guard tries to widen his split in order to set up his offensive left guard's trap block (who moves in toward his center). The center can now block back easier and pin his defender, and the trapping guard is closer to the man he is going to trap (the tackle). Similarly, the offensive right tackle moves *in* instead of out so that he can block down quickly on the middle linebacker.

Diagram 4-6 A–N illustrates 14 defensive fronts or alignments. While the offensive linemen do not have to know the spacing for all of the defenders, to be effective blockers they should be familiar with the defensive responsibilities of the personnel in their immediate area.

Diagram 4-6 A–N is also included here to illustrate how defensive fronts are numbered for identification purposes. This is basic for the most part, with certain modifications. Also basic is the information that a defensive front is either *even* or *odd,* and defenders are either head- or nose-up, inside or off-set to the outside.

Line Up Properly and Do Not Tip Off Assignment

While offensive line stance will be discussed in greater detail in Chapter 6, it is important to state here that lining up properly refers

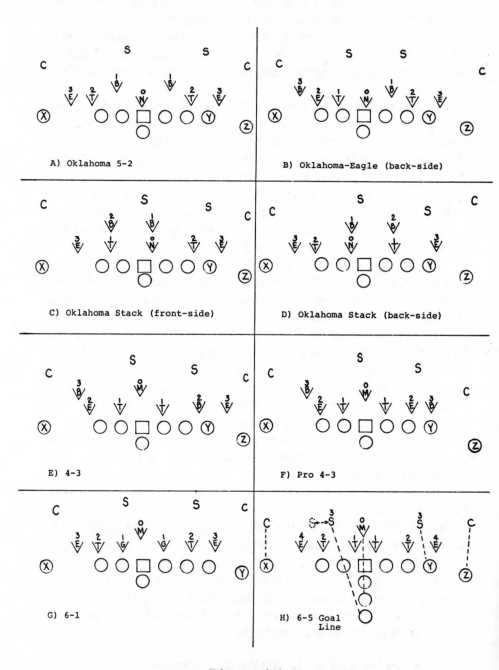

Diagram 4-6
14 defensive alignments and numbering of defensive players.

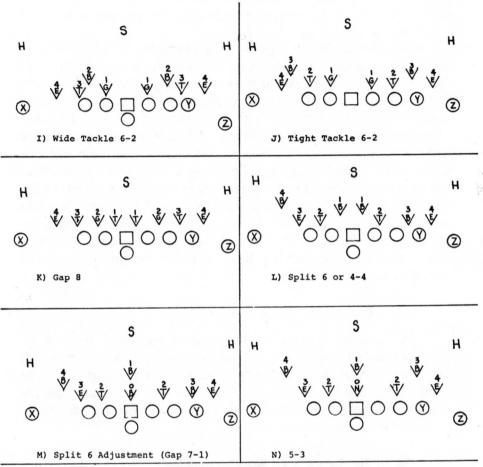

I) Wide Tackle 6-2

J) Tight Tackle 6-2

K) Gap 8

L) Split 6 or 4-4

M) Split 6 Adjustment (Gap 7-1)

N) 5-3

An offensive lineman must know the following:
(1) Offensive line splits.
(2) Defensive spacings, especially in immediate area.
(3) Who to block.

Diagram 4-6 (Contd.)

to a good stance. Fundamental to all good blocking techniques is a perfect stance, because without a good balanced stance it is difficult to start with speed, drive with power or maintain a consistent effort after the initial movements have been made.

Initial Stance Marks High Point in Form. An offensive lineman's initial stance marks the high point in form. In most instances, this form deteriorates or breaks down as the block progresses. The poorer the initial stance of the offensive lineman, the less chance he has of doing a creditable job in carrying out his assignment before the point-of-no-return is reached in his offensive block. Therefore, an offensive lineman should line up in the most perfect stance possible when he comes to the line-of-scrimmage. By taking a perfect stance, an offensive lineman does not tip off his assignment or what he intends to do. He keeps the intent of his assignment to himself, which will aid him in being a successful blocker. However, if he modifies his stance noticeably, he is tipping off the intent of his offensive assignment. Therefore, a coach must continually be on the alert for correcting tip-offs and other such faulty line play.

Block Through and Beyond the Defender

An offensive lineman should sprint to and *block through* his opponent, and should not block around the defender. Although several different points-of-view will be expressed relevant to a particular type of blocking (Chapter 6), all coaches agree with the basic principle that the blocker must *block through and beyond* his defender to be successful in executing his technique.

Never Step Laterally for Blocking Position

Through the intelligent use of offensive line splits (*see Guides for Offensive Line Splits,* Diagram 4-4), the blocker can get the blocking angle on the defender. Therefore, an offensive lineman should never step *laterally* in order to try to get the blocking angle on his opponent. The inexperienced player will not know how to employ line splits to aid him with his blocking assignment, and inevitably he will step for position when blocking. He must be taught the former, and when he does the latter, this error must be corrected.

Get Your Head Between Defender and Ball Carrier

A blocker should always drive his head or body between the critical point-of-attack or the ball carrier and the defender, and he should keep his feet out of the hole. A good blocker never looks back. He runs through the defender who is in his path. He must be coached not to run by a potential tackler in order to block another opponent farther upfield. An offensive lineman should go hard all the way, and he should "play out the play" until the whistle sounds.

Anticipate Movement by the Defender

Even when the defensive lineman or linebacker is not stunting and he is reading and reacting, the offensive blocker must anticipate movement by the defender. Certain defensive alignments, such as gaps and gap stacks, put defenders in positions where their initial movement is likely to be forward. When blocking down, such as when the defender is lining up in the inside gap, a good blocker always anticipates the forward movement of his opponent and then adjusts on his block. The reverse shoulder block will be explained in detail in Chapter 6 to illustrate this point (Diagram 6-3).

Anticipate Lateral Movement (Pursuit). The offensive blocker must anticipate the defender's lateral pursuit to the ball carrier, too. In Diagram 4-5 (left illustration), the offensive left guard must take an inside cut-off course in going after the linebacker; otherwise, the guard will be blocking behind the defender as the latter moves laterally on the flow of the play. Defenders do not remain stationary, but react to movement. Therefore, a good offensive blocker will anticipate movement (reaction) of the defender as soon as the ball is snapped.

Never Allow Penetration into the Backfield

Mention was made previously of the intelligent use of offensive line splits in order to get the blocking angle, and conversely, the danger of over-splitting, which will permit a defender to shoot the gap and get penetration into the backfield. Therefore, the blocker must not permit such deep penetration or the defender will make the big defensive play and stop the offense in its own backfield. The blocker must meet power with power. All of the techniques will be discussed in subsequent chapters, as will pass blocking techniques. To be a successful blocker, an offensive lineman cannot allow penetration into his backfield.

Sustain Your Block

Once contact has been made with the defender, the blocker must sustain pressure on him or the opponent will recover from the block. If the offensive lineman goes to the ground, he should scramble and crab his man in order to tie him up if possible, so as to keep the defensive player out of the pursuit pattern. One does not sustain contact with a defensive opponent when he attempts to use a *screen* block or a *finesse* block, which are misnomers, as a good defender is never going to be finessed or screen blocked. Only good, solid blocking is going to accomplish the job for an offensive lineman.

Synchronize Arm-Leg Movement

The offensive blocker should synchronize his arm-leg movement and pull through with the free arm to aid him in blocking, as this helps him maintain good body balance.

Use Correct Techniques or Know *How* to Block

Mention was made previously of the importance of knowing *who* to block. It is just as important to know *how* to block. Therefore, it is very important to master and habitually utilize correct blocking techniques. The correct techniques, or *how* to block, will be discussed in detail in Chapters 5–8.

There is a correct and an incorrect way of executing every blocking technique and assignment. A player should not be permitted to replace one technique with another, any more so than he should be allowed to substitute an easier blocking assignment for the designated one. While the latter illustration is an obvious error, sometimes the former is not recognized as readily. When replacing one technique with another, an offensive lineman may enjoy some success upon turning to the easy, incorrect way of carrying out his designated assignment. This is apt to be misleading, and in the final analysis will lead to trouble, in that the offensive blocker will not be consistently successful in carrying out his blocking assignment by employing incorrect techniques.

Cover All Passes

Passing game techniques for the offensive linemen will be discussed in Chapter 8. However, after a pass is thrown, the offensive linemen should always cover in the direction the ball is thrown in the event of an interception. While this is a secondary responsibility, as their primary duty is to protect the passer, probably the former is violated more than any of the others mentioned above. Interior line-men are usually involved with close-in blocking and are not cognizant of the fact that the ball has been thrown, unless the quarterback gives a release signal. Few quarterbacks remember to give a release signal for their offensive linemen to cover the pass. Secondly, it requires a disciplined offensive lineman to go head-to-head with a defender and then sprint to cover a pass, especially if it is thrown to the flat. Consequently, it is difficult to get offensive linemen to cover a pass, although it is good football to do so.

Study Your Opponent

Where rules permit film exchange between opponents, offensive linemen (in this particular instance) will gain much by studying their upcoming opponents individually. Many times films will reveal the following about a particular defender:

1. *Personal Traits*—Determination, second effort, aggressiveness, intelligence, reaction, pursuit, strength, movement, quickness, agility, speed.
2. *Playing Ability*—Skill or mechanics in using his hands, forearm lift and shiver, escaping from the trap, double-team blocks, etc. Type of charge; i.e., penetration, "reader," step-around, "water buffalo," etc.
3. *Defensive Alignments*—Loop, angle, play straight, stunt, etc.; also type of charge from these various fronts.
4. *Tip-Offs*—Crowds the ball when he is coming hard, moves off the line (in or out) when stunting (in order to get to his point or area of responsibility), changes positions of hands and/or feet and weight distribution when he is going to stunt, etc.

Regardless of the blocking techniques which will be utilized, if an offensive lineman will apply the more than a dozen principles or "musts" discussed in this chapter, he will be highly successful in carrying out his blocking assignment.

COACHING POINTS FOR TEACHING OFFENSIVE LINE TECHNIQUES

The answer to offensive failure usually lies in not having time to develop the proficiency blocking demands. In practice, the linemen generally do not spend a proportionate amount of time practicing these techniques in relation to the percentage of time they are likely to employ them in a game. The reasons for not knowing how to block might not be entirely the lineman's fault. Therefore, a coach must organize the practice schedule to give each skill an appropriate amount of teaching time.

Frequently, a player becomes discouraged over his limited success in blocking. This calls for a careful analysis of his stance and form to determine where he is encountering difficulty. In order for an offensive lineman to become proficient, he must master the techniques of blocking, know what is to be accomplished and make a determined and aggressive effort.

Analyze and Correct the Causes of Blocking Failures

The causes of blocking failures are as follows:

1. Not knowing the offensive assignment or lacking positiveness about the assignment; i.e., not knowing *who* to block or the failure of the offensive blocker to know *what* is to be accomplished.
2. Loafing or indifference about blocking assignments or proper techniques, or not knowing *how* to block.
3. Tipping off the offensive assignment.
4. Lack of aggressiveness and hustle, or the failure to make a determined and aggressive effort to carry out the blocking assignment.
5. Slow starting or inability to "get off with the count."
6. The failure to operate from a good base and football position at all times, including losing the feet after contact or failure to sustain contact.

A football axiom is, "A good football team follows the three *E*'s: *E*nthusiasm, *E*ncouragement and *E*xecution!" Therefore, as a coaching point, stress *execution,* not plays. Secondly, analyze all blocking techniques, which will be discussed in Chapters 5–8. Before doing that, however, for clarity it is necessary to first illustrate in Diagram 4-7 *a method or system* of numbering offensive holes, numbering the offensive backs and developing terminology for calling offensive plays so that the illustrations used throughout the book will be more meaningful. Since this book does not deal with either offensive or defensive systems, the discussion will be limited in scope.

A METHOD OF CALLING OFFENSIVE SIGNALS

In the offensive huddle, the quarterback will call the *formation, play number* and *starting signal.*

Formations

Diagram 4-7 (lower three illustrations) indicates three backfield sets; namely, *Split, I* and *Strong,* with the word *right* (or *left*) added to inform the offensive backs and linemen which side of the formation is *strong* or *front side*. In Split the fullback always goes strong or front side, as does the Z back in almost all formations (except when double flankers are called, Diagram 7-3; Z then goes to the side of X or *opposite* the call of "right" or "left").

The offensive linemen are not overly concerned with Split, I, or Strong, but listen for direction, right or left. If the offensive line is flip flopping, the direction given means the line will flop in that direction and the strong tackle, as an illustration, will always be the strong tackle regardless of right or left.

If *only* the tight end (Y) and split end (X) flip-flop, along with the flanker back (Z) and the running back (R), then right and left give them direction and the five interior linemen remain the same. This means the call of "right" or "left" sends Y and Z to the same side (called), and X and R (depending on the formation) go opposite the call. Since the five linemen do not flop (in this system), the right tackle is always the right tackle, although in right formation he will be the strong-side (front-side) tackle, and in the left formation he will be the weak-side (back-side) or quick tackle.

Numbering System or Play Number

In Diagram 4-7 (top illustration), the holes are numbered from inside-out, large to small, *even* to the *right, odd* to the *left*. The offensive plays are run at offensive holes over a player or area.

The backs are also numbered, as well as lettered (Diagram 4-7, bottom three illustrations). Any back behind his tackle is in a "4" position, so that in a split formation there are two "4" backs. When the fullback lines up behind his quarterback (in most formations), he is in the "3" back position. With either the running back (R) or (Z) flanker back behind the fullback, as illustrated, he is the "2" back.

A term or word added to the two numbers, such as illustrated in Diagram 4-1, Lee, Trap, Blast, Bootleg, and in Diagram 4-5, Gee or G, and Trap, indicates the type of play and the blocking scheme (which is built into the play, although the offensive linemen must apply blocking rules).

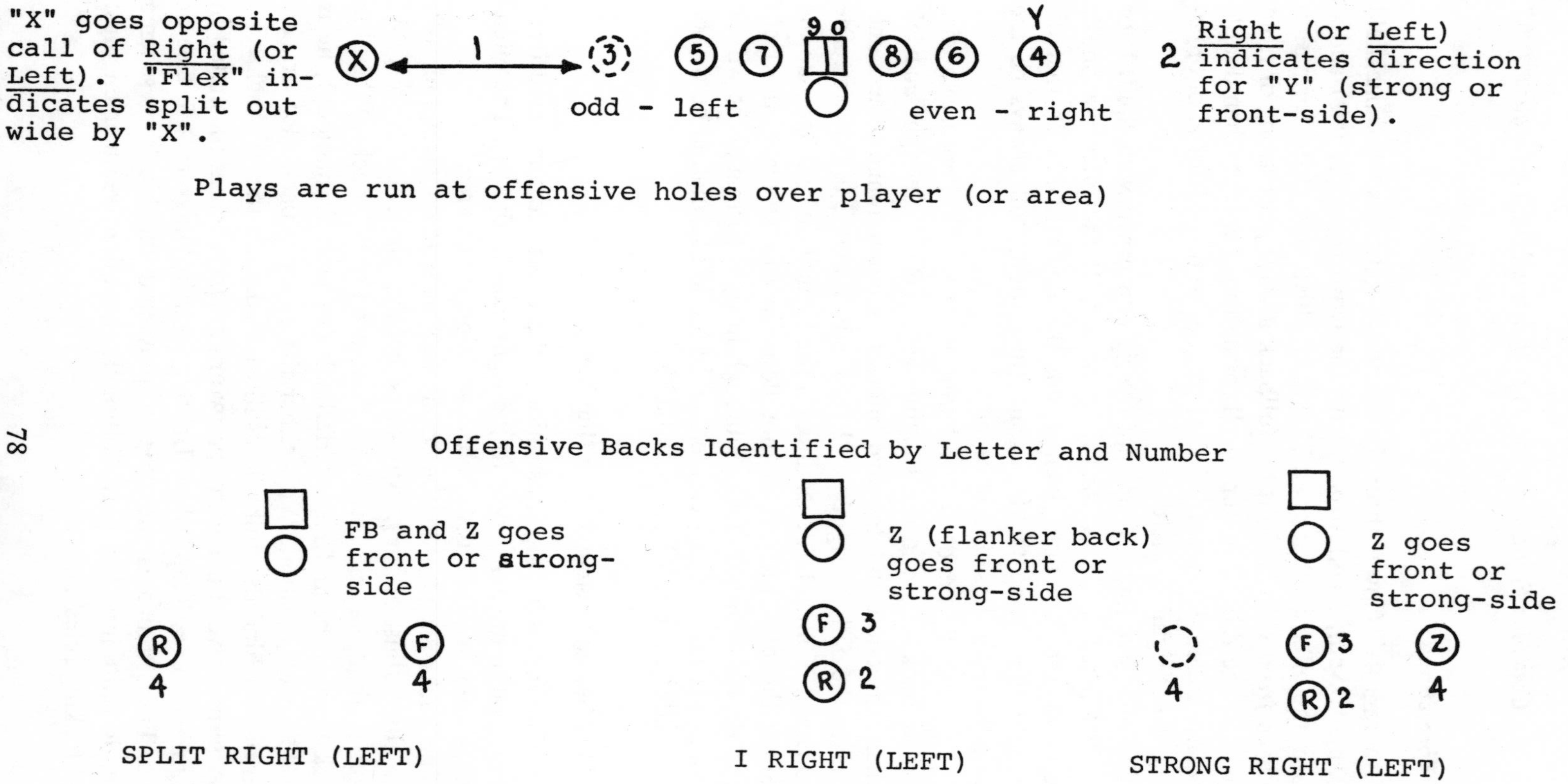

"X" goes opposite call of Right (or Left). "Flex" indicates split out wide by "X".

Right (or Left) indicates direction for "y" (strong or front-side).

2 indicates direction

odd - left   even - right

Plays are run at offensive holes over player (or area)

Offensive Backs Identified by Letter and Number

FB and Z goes front or strong-side

Z (flanker back) goes front or strong-side

Z goes front or strong-side

SPLIT RIGHT (LEFT)

I RIGHT (LEFT)

STRONG RIGHT (LEFT)

Diagram 4-7

An offensive numbering system and method of calling formations and plays.

Starting Count

The starting count may be almost anything, such as "Go," or your automatic system may be built into the starting count, too. The first example will be used, and the use of an automatic system for changing plays at the line-of-scrimmage will not be discussed further. Therefore, using the illustrations in Diagram 4-5, the quarterback would call the *formation, play number* and *starting count* in the offensive huddle as follows: "I Right, 30 Trap (Fly) on Go" or "I Right, 34 Gee (Fly) on Go." (*Fly* indicates the tailback goes *away* from the hole called; *motion* means tailback goes toward hole or play called.)

Incidentally, in Diagram 4-5, with two tight ends illustrated, the quarterback could also run these plays from I Left, 30 Trap and I Left, 34 G, with only X and Y having different assignments (if the remainder of the offensive line is not flopped).

In Diagram 4-1, the quarterback could call the plays as follows: "I Right, 28 Lee (28 Trap or 28 Bootleg) on Go" (for simplicity purposes), but he would have to call the Blast as follows, changing his formation: "Strong Right, 28 Blast on Go." These plays (except Blast) could also be run off of other formations, too, but the above diagrams will suffice for illustrative purposes.

INTRODUCTION

It is a common fallacy to select and slot the players for all of the other positions, then take the ones left over and label them "centers." A prospect cannot be relegated to the center position because he is either too slow or too small to play anywhere else. Granted the offensive center does not have to be your best athlete or prospect; however, regardless of the offensive system, the center position carries much responsibility, and you want to slot players other than the "left-overs" in this position.

Ball Exchange Must Be Fast, Hard, Accurate and Automatic

The center controls the timing of his team, and proper timing is the essence of any offense. The T-formation center will "snap back" the football to his quarterback approximately 70–75 times in a typical collegiate game. The exchange must be fast, hard, accurate and automatic. If the center does not execute the exchange properly, he can cause his team's offense to falter through fumbles, miscues and poorly timed plays. The center must be able to make the long pass to the punter in punt formation, and to the holder's hands on placement and field goal attempts. In addition, the center must be able to execute the basic fundamentals and techniques of an offensive lineman (Chapter 6).

Coaching Center Play Fundamentals, Skills and Techniques

The Advantages of Good-Sized Center Personnel

Selecting a good-sized player for the center position, who is alert, rugged and durable, is advantageous for the following reasons:

1. He can hold his own more readily with an aggressive, hard-charging defender nose-on than a small-sized center. If the defender over the center can drive him into his quarterback, or the center cannot handle him, the nose-man need not vary his tactics because he will literally stop the offense single-handed.

2. He protects his quarterback better, and the latter can "stand tall" behind a good-sized center. The quarterback is more relaxed from his high position, and he has a better view of the field and the defense.

3. He widens the offensive front, which in turn widens the territory the defense must protect, since a good-sized center takes a wider stance.

4. A center with short arms and short legs is not satisfactory because he simply cannot do the job, and does not have the physical qualifications the position demands.

Therefore, if possible, select a good-sized prospect for the center position, and preferably one who hustles. A slow center can cause the entire offense to drag if he is not enthusiastic in his play. Generally, if the center hustles, his team will hustle, too.

THE T-CENTER'S STANCE

There is no single *right* method relevant to stance and exchange of the football. The methods vary as do the reasons for teaching a particular stance and ball exchange.

With the exception of the pass for punts and placement attempts, for the most part a T-formation center makes one type of pass. The snap-back to the quarterback is very important for obvious reasons mentioned previously. The center must start with a comfortable stance from which he can carry out his duties of charging and blocking, after executing a successful snap-back.

Square Stance, Feet Even and Parallel

From a square stance with the feet even and parallel, the center can step quickly with either foot when firing out to block his opponent. Nor does a square stance present any difficulty for the center in making the exchange of the football with his quarterback. The stance should be comfortable and solid, and must afford the center freedom of movement when he is making his pass.

For the *right*-handed quarterback, the lacing on the football should be almost straight up, but slightly to the *left*. When the center places his hands on the football, it will be approximately at arm's length directly in line with his nose and the median of his body, with the lacing slightly to the *left* of center in line with his *left* eye. The long axis of the football bisects the center's nose, median of his body and crotch. The horizontal axis of the football is parallel with the line-of-scrimmage.

Individual Differences

Since there are *slight individual differences* in the manner in which quarterbacks place their hands in position to receive the football, a *slight* adjustment as to the exact positioning of the lacing becomes an individual matter to be worked out between each center and quarterback. The center places the football in the prescribed manner (lacing in line with his left eye) and adjusts from there, so that on the exchange the fingertips of the quarterback's passing (right) hand will be on the lacing immediately.

Suggested Stance

The following stance is suggested for the offensive centers:

1. Spread feet moderately (slightly wider than arm-pits), as wide apart as the center's ability to move in any direction will permit *without lowering his tail.* The feet are parallel, with the toes and heels even, in a boxed stance. Both heels are slightly *off the ground,* and the weight is on the balls of the feet.

2. The ankles and knees are flexed and on line with the stance in order to produce power in the forward charge. They are pointed straight ahead, and in line with the feet.

3. The tail and hips are slightly higher than the shoulders. They are square to the line-of-scrimmage and with the shoulders.

4. The torso is in a plane parallel with the ground, but the back may be arched slightly. The shoulders are level and squared to the line-of-scrimmage.

5. The head is tilted back straight from the shoulders. The neck is "bulled." The head is up and there is a natural extension of the

neck, but do *not* force the tail down. The eyes look straight down-field, but through peripheral vision the center sees the entire area. He should not tip off his blocking assignment with his head or eyes.

6. The right arm is straight to the football, with the right hand on the forward right side. The fingers are spread moderately in grasping the football, with the right thumb across the forward tip of the lacing. The left arm is fairly straight to the football, with the left hand on the lower left side. The fingers are spread moderately, grasping the ball with the left thumb across the rear tip of the lacing. (Slight individual differences in the placement of the hands on the football are recognized.)

7. The weight is evenly distributed on the balls of the feet. The center should not put excessive weight on the football, but tilt the nose of the ball up slightly, and push downward with his rear (left) hand rather than with his front (right) hand. He should assume a good, solid, balanced, comfortable stance in order to do his job properly.

Four-Point Center Stance. Some coaches prefer a four-point stance, teaching the center to drive the football to his quarterback's hands only with the power (right) hand on the football, and utilizing the off (left) hand to maintain body balance by placing it on the ground. Their reasoning is not illogical, and their teaching is sound. It is merely a matter of preference which method is taught and used.

If the four-point stance is preferred, the football is off-set slightly to the center's right, instead of placing it in the middle of his body as was described previously. The remaining techniques and principles are the same.

THE AUTOMATIC EXCHANGE WITH THE QUARTERBACK

Since the timing and snap-back must be perfect on the exchange, the center must know the *exact "spot"* where the quarterback places his hands so he will know where he must place the football. If the center cannot feel the quarterback's hands in his crotch at this spot, he need only say, "More pressure." The quarterback will then press upward with the back of his top (right) hand in the center's crotch. However, if the center "sits down" on his quarterback's hands, he will feel pressure.

The Conventional Exchange

In the conventional exchange, the center's right arm and hand drive the football back as fast, hard and accurately to the quarterback's top hand as possible. The center's right forearm should turn naturally to the inside, so that the right palm will be facing upward (which will be about a quarter of a turn with the football). Some coaches feel the center must lock his elbow and snap the football to the quarterback with a pendulum delivery, otherwise the football will be brought up short of the spot where the quarterback has placed his hands and a fumble will occur. Other coaches want the center to lift or *snatch* the football and *break* the elbow, turning the wrist naturally on the delivery. They feel a pendulum delivery shifts the center's weight forward (*turtle back*), inhibiting lateral movement and setting up for passes. Regardless of the technique employed, there must be consistency in the exchange. Both techniques are taught.

The left hand slides from the football naturally as the driving (right) hand delivers the ball to the quarterback's hands.

Coaching Points on the Exchange

Before enumerating a dozen reasons for ball exchange fumbles between the center and quarterback, as a coaching point teach *all* of your centers how to place their hands as the quarterback places his to receive the snap from center. Secondly, a coach should teach all of his centers and quarterbacks, including the centers who work with each other as center-quarterback, how to analyze the reason for ball exchange fumbles, so they can correct their errors. Thirdly, teach all centers to *pass and step every time*—not just pass the ball.

REASONS FOR BALL EXCHANGE FUMBLES

If the ball exchange between the center and his quarterback is not fast, hard, accurate and automatic, there is likely to be a fumble.

Regardless of when the fumble on the exchange occurs, the coach should determine and analyze why it occurred, and then correct the error so it does not happen again. Since centers and quarterbacks may not always be working under the supervision of a football coach, they should be taught to recognize and correct faulty ball exchanges. Using the previously mentioned *Suggested Stance* and the coaching points for the *Automatic Exchange with the Quarterback* as the guide or the *correct techniques*, ball exchange fumbles occur for the following reasons:

1. Center takes improper stance and exchange is inconsistent.

2. Center fails to place football properly and exchange is inconsistent.

3. Center lowers his tail upon delivery of the football and quarterback fails to *ride* center's tail with his hands.

4. Center straightens his legs upon delivery of the football and quarterback fails to *ride* center's tail with his hands.

5. Center attempts to *beat* the snap count, and seldom is a quarterback ready to receive the exchange on an "early" count.

6. Center is behind the snap count, usually as the result of trying to make a *soft,* easy exchange.

7. Center *throws* the football to the quarterback, instead of making a hand-to-hand exchange.

8. Center *twists* the football upon delivery to quarterback, instead of permitting the right forearm-wrist to turn naturally to the inside.

9. Center is inconsistent in delivering the football to the "spot," as the quarterback should always get the *fat* part of the football.

10. Quarterback pulls his hands out too soon, generally as the result of employing a *kick-out* step to get away quickly.

11. Quarterback places his hands improperly to receive the exchange in the prescribed manner.

12. Small-sized personnel at the center position. This point was discussed previously.

T-CENTER'S BLOCKING TECHNIQUES

The T-formation center can concentrate his entire attention on the opponent who is to be blocked. One distinct advantage the center has over his opponent is that he knows the starting count and his opponent does not.

Many coaches feel that blocking is mostly desire and determination on the part of the player to whip his man and get the job done. The T-formation center should know that because of the offense employed he is *not* a handicapped blocker. He should be as effective a blocker as the other offensive linemen, without making any sacrifices in the center-quarterback exchange of the football. His blocking techniques were discussed and illustrated in Chapter 6.

THE CENTER'S PUNTING GAME TECHNIQUES

It is extremely difficult to win a football game when a team has a punt blocked. While there are a number of reasons why a punt may be blocked—namely, an inaccurate pass from the center, too slow a pass from center, punter takes too long to punt, poor protection, etc.— an estimated figure is that 98 per cent of the time punts are blocked because of an imperfect pass from the center to the punter. Many teams do not use the spread punt formation because their centers cannot get the football back to the punter with speed and a fair degree of accuracy. A center's objective is to get the football back to his punter *accurately,* at 13 yards, in not more than seven-tenths of a second. To employ the spread punt formation, the punter must have a minimum depth of 13 yards from his center.

Many centers who perform well in the T-formation offense with direct snap-backs to the quarterback, and with close-in blocking in which they can see and concentrate on the opposition, are erratic when they must lower their head and pass the football to a teammate who is more than 7–8 yards behind the line. Yet the center is the vital man in the punt because he must get the football to the punter with a fairly strong pass. Therefore, the center's first responsibility is to make a good pass, and then block. Regardless of the punt formation employed, the center must be drilled thoroughly in the fundamentals and techniques of this important phase of the game.

PUNTING GAME COACHING POINTS

Before considering the stance for the center for the deep punt, let us first consider several very important teaching-coaching principles and suggestions which should be adhered to by player and coach in mastering this phase of the punting game.

Build Center's Confidence

You should teach and talk positively and confidently in working with your centers to master the long pass. Build up your centers' confidence; praise freely. Do not put a stop-watch on your centers initially, as the time element should *not* be emphasized in the beginning. Nor should you be overly concerned whether or not the football spirals initially. This will come in time as their performance improves. Confidence is very important, and as a coach you should always try to build each prospect's confidence in himself.

Mastering the Long Pass Is Simple and Easy

As a coach you should talk about how *simple* and *easy* it is for the center to make the long pass to the punter. Stress the fact that making the pass is not involved or complicated. If a player can shoot a two-handed set shot with a basketball, then he can make the long pass for the deep punt. As a suggestion, teach your centers the two-handed basketball set shot using *wrist action*. Emphasize "hanging the hands over the front rim of the basket" from 20 feet away when they shoot, as this will teach them to over-emphasize wrist action or snap. The *secret* for making the long pass for the deep punt is in the *snap* of the wrists.

Encourage Strengthening Their Weakness

Encourage your centers to work to strengthen their weakness; namely, making the deep pass to the punter as often as possible. When a center comes on the practice field, he should develop the habit of getting a football and working with anyone who is available to catch his deep punt passes. Time lost on the practice field is never regained, so make the most of the practice time.

Practice Centers Versus All Situations

A coach must make certain to drill his centers versus all situations they are likely to encounter in a game. As an illustration, the centers should practice passing the football *with* and *against* the wind, and with a wet football.

Also it is a coach's responsibility to be certain his centers get practice passing the football from inside the 3-yard line under the most adverse conditions, when it is likely the opposition will "storm the castle." Any time the football is spotted this close to the goal line, a coach must make adjustments in his punt protection since his punter cannot get the minimum 13-yard depth for punts.

Offer the Centers Some Resistance

Your center should wear his headgear all of the time, and he should encounter some type of *limited* and *controlled* resistance most of the time. Almost every time your center passes the football to his punter, he should gain some experience blocking or bumping a defender or a bag that offers some resistance. The purpose is two-fold: (1) you do not want your center watching the flight of the football on the way back to the punter; (2) it gets your center accustomed to a *limited* and *controlled* amount of bumping or jolting, which builds up his confidence. The more experience a center gains in practice under pressure, the more competent job he is likely to do during a game.

CENTER'S STANCE FOR THE LONG PASS

Most coaches favor a toe-to-instep, staggered stance for the center, with the feet wider apart than in the conventional T-stance, little weight forward on the football, most of the weight on the balls of the feet and center's eyes on the target (inside thigh of the punter's kicking leg).

Staggered Stance

Stagger the feet toe-to-instep, with the *right foot back,* in order to make the long pass for the deep punt. Some coaches teach their centers to take a staggered stance with the left foot back.

Placement of Hands on the Football

The football should be placed forward at a comfortable arm's length. For the *right-handed* center, the forward or power (right) hand should grasp the football just as if he were throwing a forward pass, with his fingers on the lacing. The bottom side of the ball will be facing upward since the lacing and the fingers will be down under, and the right wrist will be cocked slightly.

The guide (left) hand may be placed forward or parallel to the power (right) hand, or positioned on the lower rear portion of the football in the most comfortable and advantageous spot. Some coaches teach the center to make a "cocked T" with the thumbs; i.e., the thumb of the right hand (the top of the T) is across the forward tip of the football (bottom side up), and the left thumb is placed perpendicular to and bisects the right thumb (forming a T), with the fingers of the left hand pointing downward toward the lacing on the ball, too.

Regardless of the manner in which he places his hands and feet, do not make changes unless your center encounters difficulty getting the ball to his punter. The idea is to let your center get as *comfortable* as possible, and suggest changes in his stance only to aid him in making the long pass.

MAKING THE LONG PASS

Your center's arms should move in one continuous motion on the snap, although there is a difference of opinion among coaches as to the techniques which should be employed. Some coaches teach the center to drag (lightly) the football, and others teach their centers to lift the ball slightly from the ground and fire it back to the punter. In the latter technique it appears there are two motions by the center (lifting the ball, then firing it back), although coaches who teach this method contend it is done in one motion. Other coaches teach their centers to make a "clean" pass; i.e., do not drag the ball, and do not lift it as in the second technique, in one continuous motion.

Little pressure should be exerted on the football, with most of the weight on the balls of the feet. The arms should be brought through in one continuous motion, favoring the method taught by the third group of coaches; i.e., make a *clean* pass.

The Follow-Through

The legs should *not* be straightened, and the center's tail should *not* be elevated when he makes the long pass. His follow-through should be with both hands. Wrist snap must be developed to get power in the center's pass.

As the football leaves the center's hands, his first responsibility, which is to make a good pass, is ended. As was mentioned previously, the center's objective is to get the football to his punter accurately, in not more than seven-tenths of a second.

PUNTING GAME BLOCKING TECHNIQUES

The center's second responsibility is to block if there is a defender over him. The center should snap his head up immediately, keeping both eyes open, search for an opponent coming over his territory and brace himself. In most instances in both placement and punt protection, the center uses passive protection to the extent he makes the defender come to him rather than firing out aggressively (and never blindly). In punt protection, the center generally releases downfield when he is not covered. Otherwise the center should protect his territory, using a pass protection block. He should maintain a good football position and have good balance.

SELECTED DRILLS REFERENCE*

(*See* footnote source for 13 football drills for teaching center play fundamentals, skills and techniques, although the previously mentioned "Coaching Points" are probably just as important and beneficial as the drills.)

---

* Donald E. Fuoss, *Championship Football Drills for Teaching Offensive and Defensive Fundamentals and Techniques* (Englewood Cliffs, N.J.: Prentice-Hall, Inc., 1964), pp. 103-107, 185.

INTRODUCTION

It is impossible to move the football offensively if a team does not have sound blocking techniques. Blocking must be taught in a logical manner to attain maximum results. These fundamental ideas dictate the types of blocks linemen must use to handle their offensive assignments. Therefore, a coach must determine the fundamental requisites of every good blocking maneuver and teach these first. Fundamental to all good blocking movements is a *perfect stance,* regardless of the various types of blocks used. The stance is the first consideration for line instruction and practice. Good execution begins with a well-balanced stance, from which a lineman must be able to charge forward or to either side with equal ability, speed and power, and never indicate which movement he is apt to make.

OFFENSIVE LINE STANCE

There is little value in teaching the elements of the various blocks unless a solid base is provided. Without a good, balanced stance, it is difficult to start with speed, drive with power or maintain a consistent effort after the initial movements have been made. A correct stance will promote a balanced position during the interval between starting and contact. If the offensive blocker does not start from a good position, then some advantage is being sacrificed immediately.

Coaching Offensive Interior Line Fundamentals, Skills and Techniques

Stance Depends on Type of Offense Utilized

Just as the type of offense dictates the blocking techniques, it also determines the most advantageous stance the offensive player should assume. If the line blocking is primarily 1-on-1, a "go get 'em and stay after 'em" offense, then it is better for the offensive linemen to utilize a four-point stance with more weight forward on the hands. A four-point stance lowers the center of gravity of the offensive blocker and permits more straight-ahead explosion in his block, as it permits a quicker start. Its appearance also gives the offensive line a more aggressive "hard-nosed look," and there is no tipping or pointing in a four-point stance.

If a coach's offensive philosophy is to throw the football, especially using drop-back passing, and/or he employs a pulling-trapping type of offensive ground attack, then it is better for his offensive linemen to assume a three-point stance. The latter permits more freedom of movement in carrying out the various types of blocking techniques than does a four-point stance.

Recognize Individual Differences

Stance is important in an offensive lineman's ability to carry out his assignment; therefore, a coach must take into consideration individual physical differences of his linemen. Consideration should be given to seeking naturalness in a player's stance, as well as comfort and maneuverability. Individual physical deviations as to height and length of arms and legs should be taken into consideration, and no attempt should be made to stereotype exactly one stance for all linemen. What might be the perfect stance for one lineman might not be the best stance for another. However, the basic fundamentals listed below are sound and may be used as the basis for a good offensive line stance.

Three-Point Offensive Line Stance Fundamentals

The fundamentals of a three-point offensive line stance (*right-handed*) are as follows:

1. Feet should be approximately hip (outside) width or as wide as the offensive lineman's ability to move in any direction will permit; i.e., a *natural* distance apart.
2. Feet should be parallel, toes pointing straight ahead, and stag-

gered heel-to-toe—no more stagger than heel and toe and no less than toe and instep for interior linemen. The heel of the forward (left) foot will be raised slightly, and the heel of the rear (right) foot will be several inches from the ground. The ankles and knees are flexed and on line with the stance.

3. Extended (right) arm should be straight from the shoulder to the ground and slightly inside of the (right) knee, with the fingers of the (right) hand extended and the forward weight balanced on the fingertips, *not* on the knuckles. This aids in pushing off when pulling out of the line. The other (left) arm is the *adjusted* arm, and is placed in such a manner *below* the knee-cap so that the shoulders are level and square to the line-of-scrimmage. If the left arm is placed on the left thigh near the knee-cap, hand clenched and arm bent at the elbow close to a 90 degree angle, it is extremely difficult for the blocker to keep his shoulders level. (For a *left-handed stance* for the offensive lineman, the procedure for hands and feet is reversed.)

4. Hips, back and shoulders should be on the same plane, and not twisted or humped, although the tail is likely to be slightly higher than the shoulders, with the neck "bulled," and the head is tilted slightly upward. The eyes look straight ahead, but see the entire area through peripheral vision.

5. The player's weight should be distributed equally between his feet, with slight to moderate weight being placed on his down hand. The offensive lineman cannot tip off his intention by leaning in any direction, nor should he do so with his head or eyes.

Four-Point Offensive Line Stance Fundamentals

By placing the left arm in an adjusted position *below* the knee-cap (until the shoulders are level and square), the blocker is in a modified four-point stance. Therefore, if a coach desires a four-point stance, all the offensive blocker need do is place his left hand on the ground in the same manner as his right hand.

Additional fundamentals of a four-point offensive line stance are as follows:

1. The amount of weight forward on the hands depends on the extent to which the offensive lineman pulls out, trap blocks and employs drop-back pass protection.

2. The weight should be over the balls of the feet.

3. The knees are over the feet.

4. The hips are level with the shoulders, with the latter squared to the ground.

5. The head is up and the eyes are open, and the offensive lineman's body should feel like a "coiled spring."

FUNDAMENTAL BLOCKING TECHNIQUES FOR LINEMEN

The following are fundamental blocks for linemen: butt (option), drive or straight shoulder, reverse shoulder, hook, reach, scramble or crab, double-team, lead-post or power block, cut-off, seal, switch or cross-block, trap and pass blocking. All will be discussed here shortly, with the exception of pass blocking (Chapter 8).

Since most blocks originate from the basic shoulder block, it is advisable to teach its techniques first. Then you teach the other blocks, *and the situations in which each block should be utilized.* First, however, let us clarify several different points-of-view relevant to teaching blocking techniques.

DIFFERENT THEORIES ON TEACHING
LINE BLOCKING TECHNIQUES

While the inexperienced coach is likely to recognize that all coaches do not utilize the same terminology, he fails to recognize there are different theories and methods of teaching the *same* technique. A case in point is the teaching of offensive line blocking techniques, which for the sake of organization will be identified and presented as: (a) opposite foot/opposite shoulder techniques and (b) near (same) foot/near (same) shoulder techniques.

Opposite Foot/Opposite Shoulder–
Near Foot/Near Shoulder Techniques

Diagram 6-1 (A) illustrates the "step out" blocking technique, or as it is commonly known, the *opposite (on) foot/opposite (off) shoulder technique;* Diagram 6-1 (B) illustrates the same foot/same shoulder or the *near (off) foot/near (off) shoulder blocking technique* versus the defender nose-on.

The *off, on, far* and *near* terminology may also confuse the inexperienced coach even further because the terms are not used by all coaches in the same manner and with the same degree of consistency;

although, as a point-of-reference they generally refer to *toward* and *away* from the point-of-attack. The same terms may change in their interpretation at times, too, depending on whether the defender is *on* the line as a down lineman or *off* the line as a linebacker, and whether the defender is head-on or off-set outside or inside the blocker's position, all of which are predicated on the point-of-attack.

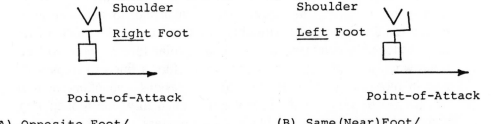

Left Shoulder Block

Diagram 6-1
Straight shoulder blocking techniques.

While it is important for the coach to know and understand what should be taught, it is more important for the players to understand what the coach is teaching. Therefore, the most easily understood terminology in this instance is to refer to the linemen's feet as *right, left, inside foot* and/or *outside foot*. While the coaches who advocate techniques (A) and (B) (Diagram 6-1) each feel *theirs* is the *best*, this is of little concern to offensive linemen. It is very important that the players learn to execute to the *best* of their ability the method which is taught and not get confused with the terminology.

Illustrating Both Theories, Employing a Shoulder Block. In Diagram 6-1 (A) and (B), the offensive lineman (center) will execute a *left* shoulder block, getting his head to the right side of the defender since the point-of-attack is to the right. However, in (A), opposite foot/opposite shoulder technique, the blocker would jab step with his *outside* (right) foot first; in (B), same foot/same shoulder technique, he jab steps with his *inside* (left) foot first.

At Times It's Difficult to Differentiate Between Two Theories. At times it is difficult to differentiate between the offensive line blocking theories. Yet each line coach who advocates either method (A) or (B) insists he has conformity and consistency in teaching offensive line blocking techniques his way. However, if method (B) is taught versus the defender over the blocker *on* the line-of-scrimmage as illustrated in Diagram 6-1 (B), the same coach is likely to teach method (A) versus the defender over the blocker *off* the line-of-scrimmage (which would be the same as illustrated in Diagram 6-1 (A), even though the defender is *on* the line).

A third group of coaches advocate a more practical theory; namely, do not worry the blocker about which foot to step with first. Permit the lineman to step with either foot, as long as the blocker gets the job done. In commenting on this particular theory, there will be times when it makes little difference which foot a lineman steps with first in blocking a defender. On other occasions, the offensive line coach must be very specific in teaching a lineman which foot to step with first in order to aid the blocker with his task of blocking an opposing lineman. Finally, if the lineman does not "get the job done" after trying the third method, he must then be taught either of the first two methods.

Advantages-Disadvantages. Those coaches who advocate teaching method (A) feel the opposite foot/opposite shoulder principles aid the blocker in adjusting his blocking to pick up slanting and stunting defenders with greater effectiveness. They also feel the short jab or position (balance) step with the opposite foot permits the blocker to strike with force and power when he shoulder (slams) blocks on his second step.

Conversely, those coaches who advocate teaching method (B) feel by stepping quickly with the near (same) foot and blocking with the near (same) shoulder, the blocker gets into and makes contact with the defender before he loops, slants or stunts. These coaches feel their linemen get off the football more quickly than if a step-out technique is employed.

Recognize the Different Theories of Teaching Techniques. No attempt will be made to pursue and develop both methods (A) and (B) in their entirety throughout the remainder of this section on offensive line play, as this would lead to further confusion. The important point is for a coach to recognize there are different methods of teaching line blocking techniques. Each coach must be cognizant of the fact that there are different theories, analyze each thoroughly and then adopt and teach the techniques which he feels are the most practical to him.

Butt Versus Shoulder Block Technique

A second issue, which also tends to confuse the young coach, is whether to teach the butt (option) block or the shoulder block? However, this issue can be resolved easier because *both* techniques should be taught. It is impractical to butt block the defender on *all* occasions, and the offensive lineman *must* shoulder block his opponent when the latter is off-set.

Pros and Cons. Coaches who advocate teaching a *shoulder* block in a head-on situation aim with the head but lead and slam with the shoulder in blocking the defender. Coaches who advocate the *butt* block feel if the blocker aims with his shoulder, he will usually end up blocking with his arm. Since the arm can be bent downward, it is not an effective block. However, those who teach the butt block advocate that by hitting with the front of the helmet at the hairline, upon contact, the head will slide to one side or the other and the blocker will now have the defender on the nape of his neck and shoulder, which provides a good blocking surface. Continual contact with the defender is maintained on the follow-through.

In the *option* block the offensive lineman drives his forehead into the defender's fold, and the ball carrier reads his block and breaks off of it. The offensive lineman takes the defender in any direction he can, or any way the defender wants to go. Although this may not provide a pre-determined hole at the point-of-attack, the ball carrier has the option of breaking off of his lineman's block, which proves to be more effective many times. The blocker may have a pre-conceived idea of the direction he wants to block the defender. However, if the offensive lineman cannot accomplish this objective, he has the option of taking his opponent any way that he can as long as he opens the hole. Oftentimes this type of block ends up as a stalemate, with the blocker not moving the defender back or laterally to any appreciable extent, but positioning himself between the defender and the point-of-attack. It is for this reason that many coaches do not teach the option block as such, but advocate a straight shoulder block in order to drive the defender away from the designated point-of-attack. However, as was mentioned previously, while the butt block may be considered best in some situations, in others the offensive lineman must employ a specified shoulder block.

STRAIGHT SHOULDER OR DRIVE BLOCK TECHNIQUES

The most important block an offensive lineman must master is the straight shoulder block. The offense's success depends on it. In teaching blocking techniques, consider the *approach, contact* and *follow-through* sequence. Commence the initial move by pushing off of the big toe, using the thigh and calf muscles only. Do not change the upper body, cock the arms or dip the head or shoulders. The rear leg applies most of the drive. The forward knee flexes, rolling over with forward motion. Maintain the same elevation and head position.

In the carriage of the body, maintain the motion by straight-line action of the legs about the width of the hips. Do not swing the head or roll the shoulders or hips. Keep the height position of the body as close to the stance as possible for fast movement.

Approach/Contact/Follow-Through

In the approach, in taking the initial jab step, assume the position of the stance, keep the eyes open and strive for an *inside-out* position. The initial step must be short so that the original angles between the knee and the ankle joint are maintained.

Offensive linemen should be taught to move the shoulder and foot together so that both parts of the blocker's body are advancing across the line-of-scrimmage simultaneously.

In order to get through the defender's block protection, the initial contact must be low in the fold (above the crotch and below the belt in the defender's vulnerable area). Place the same foot as the hitting shoulder close to the opponent for contact. The shoulders, back and head are the same as in the stance. The arm on the side of the hitting shoulder should come up in the "flipper" position. The two hitting actions are as follows: (1) rolling off the forward foot, holding all parts of the body in readiness; (2) explosion on contact by the extension of the shoulders, driving off the forward knee. The extension of the shoulders is timed by the action of the forearm in a straight line about 6 inches from the opponent. The head should not turn. The off-leg comes up and outside to start the turn. The off-hand extends forward and low past the defender in order to turn the shoulders. The back should be extended to a straight position.

On the follow-through, the back remains straight and the off-leg exerts the pressure to turn the opponent. Employ a short step, with the near leg up, landing under the hip, in order to maintain pressure on the defender. Use longer steps with the off-foot and leg to the outside of the hips, exerting the strongest drive on the opponent. Squeeze the head into him, holding with the head, and look up the defender's back to his opposite shoulder. Rigidity in the upper body should be maintained. Contact should be sustained until the whistle blows.

The Difference Between a Fair and Great Blocker. The difference between a fair blocker and a great one is the fractional time between contact and drive. The usual techniques of using short, driving steps, keeping the tail lower than the shoulders, hitting, lifting and sustaining contact with the defender until the whistle blows, are all employed in the straight shoulder block. While there may be individual differences of opinion among coaches as to straight shoulder (and other) blocking techniques, all agree on the necessity of getting to the defender quickly in order to make contact and stop his penetration.

Straight Shoulder (Definite Angle) or Pin Block Techniques

Diagram 6-2 illustrates a straight shoulder block versus an even defense, where the offensive lineman (center) has a definite angle on the defender.

Most coaches would teach the center in Diagram 6-2 to step with his *near* (left) foot and block with his near (left) shoulder, which would be method (B) discussed previously. Other coaches would teach the blocker to jab step (cross over) with his *far* (right) foot first, and block with his near (left) shoulder, which would be method (A) discussed previously. The blocker's head goes behind the defender (or head into defender's ribs), with the offensive lineman running through his opponent.

Those coaches who teach method (A) feel that this situation, where the blocker has a definite angle on his opponent, conforms with the straight shoulder block as taught in Diagram 6-1 (A) versus the odd alignment, and there is no loss of striking power. Obviously these coaches feel there is a loss of striking power when method (B) is

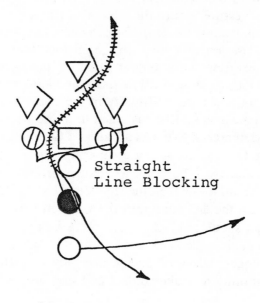

Straight
Line Blocking

30 Trap

Diagram 6-2
Straight shoulder (definite angle) or pin block–trap block techniques (30 trap).

taught. In *both* methods, the first step is a short, diagonal jab step in the direction of the defender.

The trapping and pulling techniques for the guard, and the techniques of blocking a linebacker, as illustrated in Diagram 6-2 (and in others), will be discussed shortly.

REVERSE OR OPPOSITE SHOULDER BLOCK TECHNIQUES

The reverse or opposite shoulder block is used when the offensive lineman must block down or back on a defender who is inside of the blocker's position, and who is attempting to penetrate on his charge (Diagram 6-3). The offensive blocker must adhere to the fundamental principles of blocking and the shoulder block techniques mentioned previously, with several exceptions noted.

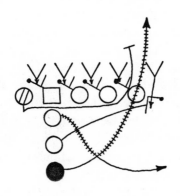

24 Power

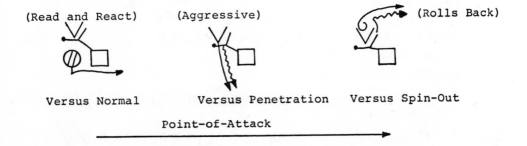

(Read and React)   (Aggressive)   (Rolls Back)

Versus Normal   Versus Penetration   Versus Spin-Out

Point-of-Attack

Diagram 6-3
Reverse or opposite shoulder block techniques (24 power).

Approach/Contact/Follow-Through

The initial step with the near (inside) foot is most important, as the blocker must step diagonally toward the defender, pointing his toe at the defender's crotch, and gain ground both forward and laterally. The head is driven in *front* of the defender's body toward his far knee, in order to check the forward progress and penetration of the defensive man. With his far arm up in a flexed position, the offensive lineman has a full blocking surface from the nape of his neck to the point of his elbow. The defender's forward movement must be redirected laterally (away from the point-of-attack) and parallel to the line-of-scrimmage with this driving (opposite shoulder) block. After contact is made, the blocker utilizes the same type of leg-drive action as was explained for the straight shoulder block techniques.

Versus the Penetrating Charge. Versus an aggressive penetrating charge (middle illustration, Diagram 6-3), the blocker continues to scramble and crab his opponent in the direction of the latter's initial charge. He merely ties up his opponent, walls off the defender and forces him to chase the play from behind.

Versus the Roll-Back Reaction of the Defender. If the defender tries to roll back or pivot out (right illustration, Diagram 6-3), the blocker must bring up his far (right) leg in an effort to tie up the defender's legs. The offensive blocker must continue to scramble and crab, and keep leverage on the defender, and he should *not* illegally clamp (hold) his opponent.

In Diagram 6-3 (top illustration), the offensive center, right guard, tackle and end all employ the reverse or opposite shoulder block in order to stop offensive penetration since the point-of-attack is outside of their respective positions. The offensive left guard is pulling behind his center in order to seal off pursuit from the inside. He steps first with his lead or near (right) foot. The remainder of the technique will be discussed shortly.

CROSS-BLOCK TECHNIQUES

Cross-blocking is an important technique which may be employed between adjacent linemen using straight shoulder and reverse shoulder blocks, and is an effective means of improving blocking angles in order to open a hole in the defensive line. In Diagram 6-4, the offensive right tackle and guard exchange blocking assignments. The right tackle must execute a reverse shoulder block. The offensive right guard drop steps with his outside (right) foot first and opens out at an angle, in order to clear his tackle and permit the latter to go in front of him. The guard then utilizes a straight shoulder block, with his head behind the defender. Both shoulder blocking techniques were explained previously.

G or Gee Block Techniques

In Diagram 6-5, with the defender (linebacker) off the line and the offensive right tackle blocking down on him, the blocker would use a straight shoulder block. In order to get through to his inside, he should step with his inside (left) foot first. Otherwise, he would probably get knocked off by the defensive left tackle, and not get

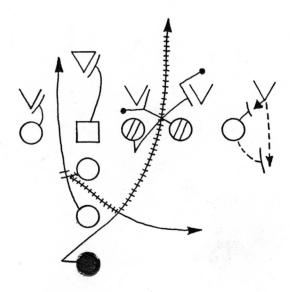

26 Counter

Diagram 6-4
Cross-block techniques (26 counter).

through on the linebacker if he were to step with his outside (right) foot first.

The offensive right end (Diagram 6-5) would utilize a reverse (right) shoulder block. The techniques have been explained previously.

The offensive right guard would pull and right shoulder block the defensive end out, with his head going behind the defender. The techniques of pulling linemen will be discussed shortly.

Fold or Switch Blocking Techniques

Another example of cross-blocking is illustrated in Diagram 6-6, which involves a switch between the offensive right guard and tackle which is somewhat different from the cross-blocking illustrated previously. While the right tackle blocks down with a reverse (right) shoulder block on the defensive tackle using the techniques described previously, the offensive right guard must *read* his inside linebacker's

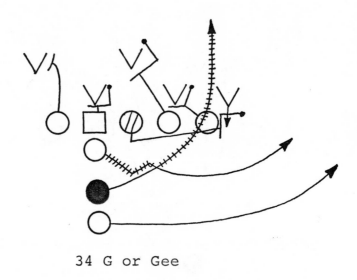

Diagram 6-5
Cross-block techniques (34 gee).

course of pursuit to the football. The latter will be reading flow, and unless he fires on a pre-determined stunt, he will attempt to run, throw or scrape off on flow to his side (Diagram 6-6). In the *left* illustration, the guard will attempt to seal off inside the scrape-off linebacker with a cut or long body block, getting his body between the defender and the point-of-attack outside. In the *right* illustration, with the point-of-attack inside the offensive end's position, the guard will probably end up driving the scrape-off linebacker *beyond* the hole with a straight shoulder block as he fills the hole, if he cannot seal off the defender to the inside.

TECHNIQUES FOR BLOCKING LINEBACKERS

A straight shoulder block technique is generally utilized to block a linebacker. Speed is essential in getting to the defender, since he will react more quickly than a defender on the line-of-scrimmage. The blocker's target is slightly higher—the bottom of the numerals on the defender's jersey—since the latter will be in a semi-upright stance. The

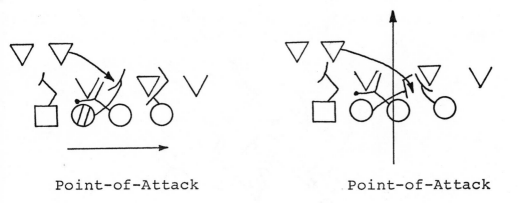

Point-of-Attack   Point-of-Attack

Diagram 6-6
Fold or switch block techniques.

offensive lineman should not over-stride or lunge at the linebacker he is to block, but should drive through him after contact is made. Getting to the linebacker quickly and then continuing to move the feet after contact is made, are probably the most important coaching points.

Cut-Off or Shoulder Blocking the Inside Linebacker

The techniques for the tackle blocking down on the Oklahoma 5-2 linebacker, illustrated in Diagram 6-5, have been discussed already. The same applies for the offensive guard pulling behind his tackle to block the scrape-off linebacker in Diagram 6-6.

Diagram 6-2 illustrates the offensive right guard *straight line* blocking down on the middle linebacker with a left shoulder block, utilizing the same techniques as the right tackle in Diagram 6-5. (*Line calls* by the offensive right guard to his right tackle indicate whether the former can get through on a straight line to the middle linebacker or whether he will *influence,* as illustrated in Diagram 6-7, which sends the right tackle down on the middle linebacker and the guard cross-blocking the adjacent defender outside.)

The offensive right tackle (Diagram 6-7) utilizes a straight (left) shoulder block; the right guard, a right shoulder block. The center blocks back with a straight (left) shoulder block. These techniques

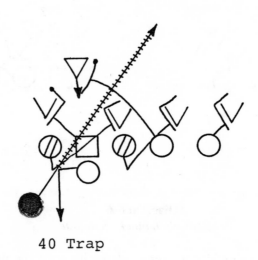

40 Trap

Diagram 6-7
Influence blocking techniques (40 trap).

have been explained previously. The offensive left guard's short trap (right) shoulder block will be explained shortly.

Diagram 6-4 illustrates a lead or cut-off (left) shoulder block by the center versus the 6-1 (4-3) middle linebacker. The offensive right guard utilizes the same technique versus the Oklahoma 5-2 alignment (Diagrams 6-12 and 6-14). With the critical point-of-attack to the outside (right), the offensive blocker steps with his outside (right) foot first, trying to get to a collision point where the flow of the offensive play (right) is likely to take the inside linebacker. The blocker should inside (left) shoulder block the linebacker, and get his head to the outside (right) between the defender and the critical point-of-attack. In addition to the previously mentioned illustrations above, the same technique would be utilized by the center in Diagrams 6-9 (middle illustration) and 6-13, and by the offensive left guard in Diagrams 6-12 and 6-13.

Butt or Option Blocking the Inside Linebacker

If the play were a quick-hitting buck or drive up-the-middle (Diagram 6-8), then the center would aggressively butt block the middle linebacker and permit the ball carrier to break off his block. This technique has been discussed already. If it were a draw play, the center would step back with either foot first, show pass blocking, then fire out and butt block the linebacker. Other draw blocking techniques versus down linemen will be discussed in Chapter 8.

Diagram 6-8
Butt or option block techniques (39 buck).

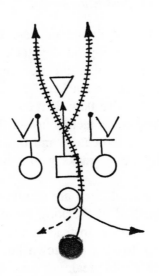

39 Buck

Cut-Off or Shoulder Blocking the Outside Linebacker

In Diagram 6-6 (left illustration), the offensive right end blocks down on the outside linebacker with a straight (left) shoulder block as the point-of-attack is outside the right end's position. Since the linebacker is inside and is a threat to fire, most coaches would teach the blocker to step with his inside (left) foot first. If the blocker reads the linebacker firing, he would attempt to drive his head in front of the defender and execute a reverse or opposite (right) shoulder block. Both shoulder block techniques have been discussed previously.

In Diagram 6-6 (right illustration) the point-of-attack is inside the right end's position. Therefore, the blocker must work for an *inside-out* position on the linebacker, stepping first with his inside (left) foot, and blocking with his outside (right) shoulder, walling off the defender to the outside away from the inside point-of-attack, if possible. These blocking techniques were explained previously.

In Diagram 6-7, with the linebacker *outside* of the offensive right end's position, and the point-of-attack inside as illustrated, the blocker would employ a straight (right) shoulder block, utilizing either technique (A) or (B), both of which have been explained previously.

Blocking the Stacked Alignment

Blocking the stacked alignment presents a problem, depending on how the opposition is playing off the stack. In Diagram 6-9 (left and middle illustrations), the down linemen are attempting to get penetration on their charge and the stacked linebackers are running through on the direction of offensive flow. If the scouting report indicates your opposition plays their stack techniques in this manner, then by numbering the defenders as indicated, and by reach blocking (which will be discussed shortly), the stacks would be blocked as indicated in Diagram 6-9.

However, if the stack men are stunting as in Diagram 6-9 (right illustration), one method of blocking the stunt would be as the right guard and tackle are doing. Instead of reach blocking, *both* offensive linemen step directly toward the down lineman with their *near* foot, just as if they were double-teaming him. One blocker picks up the down defender stunting into his area, and the other adjusts on his second step to pick up the linebacker firing into his area. In Diagram 6-9 (right illustration) versus the stunt indicated, the right tackle (left) shoulder blocks the down lineman immediately because the latter is looping or slanting into his area. The offensive right guard steps toward the down lineman, too, but adjusts on his second step when he notes the down defender stunting away from his position. The right guard then picks up (left shoulder block) the linebacker firing into his area on his pre-determined stunt.

If the stunt were vice versa with the linebacker going outside and the down lineman looping inside, the stunt would be blocked the same as the center illustration, with the right guard picking up the down

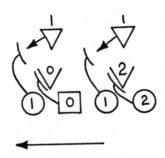

Point-of-Attack

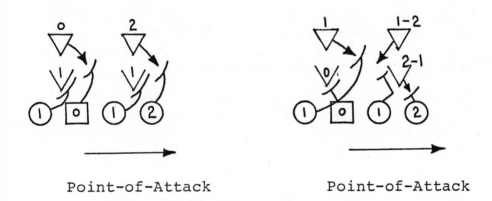

Point-of-Attack Point-of-Attack

Diagram 6-9
Blocking the stacked alignment techniques.

defender coming into his area and the right tackle adjusting on his second step to pick up the stacked linebacker firing to his side.

The blocking of the left guard and center in Diagram 6-9 (right illustration) versus a stacked alignment illustrates another blocking scheme where the center blocks #0 and the left guard blocks #1 regardless, with the point-of-attack to the right. If the point-of-attack were to the left, the center must reach block #0, and the left guard blocks #1, as indicated in Diagram 6-9 (left illustration).

Utilize an Automatic System at the Line-of-Scrimmage. The best strategy versus the stacked alignments is to utilize an automatic system at the line-of-scrimmage in order to avoid running a bad play, and to call plays which will exploit the inherent weakness of the stacked alignment. Such a discussion is outside the scope of this book.

Blocking the Off-Side Linebacker

Diagrams 6-10 and 6-11 illustrate the center blocking the off-side linebacker in the Wide Tackle 6-2 alignment, with no defender over the offensive center. However, note his techniques are different depending upon his offensive left guard's assignment.

In Diagram 6-10 the left guard (left) shoulder blocks the down lineman over him and the left tackle releases downfield. Therefore, the center would step with his outside (right) foot first and release straight out, rather than stepping with his inside (left) foot first, as in Diagram 6-11, in order to permit his off-side blocking (left tackle) to clear him (the center). If the center were to block back immediately, as is his technique in Diagram 6-11, with his tackle cutting off or sealing inside instead of releasing downfield as in Diagram 6-10, the center and tackle would be on a collision course.

Diagram 6-10
Blocking the off-side linebacker techniques.

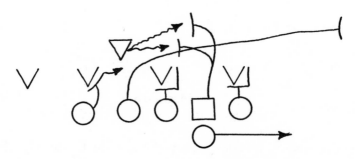

Point-of-Attack

When the Off-Guard Pulls Out. In Diagram 6-11, although the center's assignment is the same, namely to block the off-side linebacker, when the off- (left) guard pulls out, the center steps first with his near (left) foot in the event the defender pinches or stunts to the inside. Should this occur, the blocker (center) slams into the down lineman with a pin or straight (left) shoulder block, and then goes on through for the linebacker. This permits the offensive left tackle to cut off the down lineman. If the center were to release straight out (Diagram 6-10) and his guard pulls out (Diagram 6-11), if the defensive down lineman was to stunt inside, the offensive left tackle could not block him. The defender would be in the backfield almost immediately on the snap of the football.

Diagram 6-11
Sweep action—guards pull/blocking the off-side linebacker techniques (42 sweep).

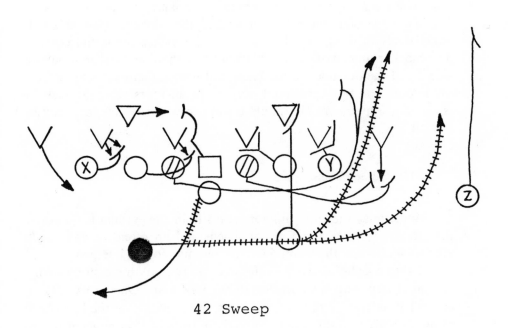

42 Sweep

REACH AND HOOK BLOCK TECHNIQUES

Reach and/or hook block techniques are utilized when the defender and the point-of-attack are outside of the offensive blocker's position. The latter must "reach" or hook the defender in order to keep him out of pursuit. Some coaches use these two terms synony-mously and interchangeably, and other coaches consider the two as separate blocking techniques. While the objective of both blocks is the same, the differences of techniques will be noted.

Reach Block Techniques

In Diagram 6-9 (left and middle illustrations), all of the offen-sive linemen are reach blocking in the direction of the point-of-attack. In both illustrations, the offensive blockers utilize a lead step directly toward the defender at an adjacent angle with the line-of-scrimmage. Most coaches teach a *lead* step first (foot nearest the defender) and driving the *far* shoulder into the defender's far (outside) knee. Other coaches teach stepping with the *far* foot first, utilizing a cross-over step. The remainder of the technique is the same, as described above.

The first step must be quick, and the blocker must scramble aggressively to tie up the defender after he makes the initial contact. The blocker must work to get his head and shoulders beyond the out-side leg of the defender so the latter will have difficulty pursuing from inside-out. The blocker should only go to all fours when he feels he is losing his opponent. He should try to run with the defender, cutting him off.

Hook Block Techniques

Sometimes the only differentiation is in the terminology, where the interior linemen *reach* an opponent and an offensive end *hooks* his defender—and the techniques are the same for all linemen.

Other coaches teach the offensive end to hook his man by taking his initial step with his outside (right) foot first (Diagram 6-12). It is a quick, lateral, slightly forward step, just enough for the blocker to bring his body to a slight angle directly in front of his opponent if pos-sible. The blocker then swings into his opponent's outside leg at knee level with his inside shoulder. It is practically impossible for the offen-sive blocker to drive the defender, as his objective should be to tie up his opponent and not permit the latter to pursue to the football imme-diately.

Diagram 6-12 illustrates the quick flip to the split back, where the end utilizes a hook block.

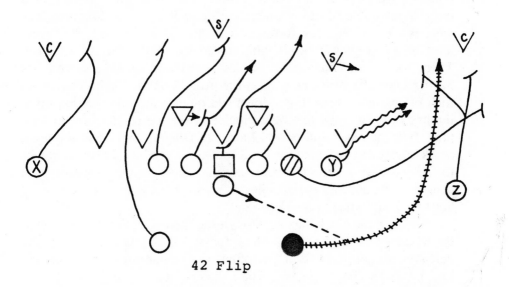

42 Flip

Diagram 6-12
Tight end (Y) employs hook block techniques (42 flip).

SCRAMBLE AND CRAB BLOCK TECHNIQUES

The scramble and crab blocks are similar to each other, just as the reach and hook blocks are similar, and in all of them after contact is made, aggressive pressure must be sustained on the opponent for the block to be executed successfully.

Just as in reach and hook, some coaches use the terms scramble and crab synonymously and interchangeably, and others consider them as separate blocks.

Scramble Block Techniques

While a blocker should scramble and stay with his opponent once contact is made, the scramble block as such is not taught as extensively now as previously. The block originated previously from the four-point stance, and the offensive lineman stayed after the defender all the way on all fours. Presently more teams probably employ a three-point, rather than a four-point stance. The latter stance lends itself more to scramble blocking than the three-point stance. Secondly, the emphasis in present-day football is on the passing game; therefore, most teams employ a three-point stance for their offensive linemen. Then, too, most coaches emphasize speed and quickness, and not having their offensive linemen on the ground on all fours. They want their offensive linemen to get downfield quickly, and not be tied up at the line-of-scrimmage scramble blocking. Yet the reach block in Diagram 6-9, the reach and cut-off blocks in Diagram 6-11 and the hook block illustrated in Diagram 6-12, are all scramble and crab blocks to the extent that pressure must be maintained on the defender once contact is made, and the blocker stays after the defender even if he must go to all fours to sustain contact.

A scramble block may be either a shoulder or option block, except the blocker generally ends up on all fours, scrambling to stay after the defender. As an illustration, the offensive lineman fires out to block a low, hard-charging opponent. The blocker's head slides under the defender's block protection into the latter's groin or stomach, and the offensive lineman then scrambles on hands and feet in order to follow through and keep pressure on his opponent. Initially the blocker might have executed a shoulder block but lost contact slightly, and he ends up on all fours, scrambling to keep his opponent engaged.

Crab Block Techniques

The old style crab or long body block is not taught as such presently, probably with the exception of employing it in conjunction with the reverse shoulder block. As was pointed out previously (Diagram 6-3, right illustration), if the defender tries to roll back or pivot out from the reverse shoulder block, then the off-leg is driven behind the defender's knees and the blocker crabs and scrambles to keep pressure on his opponent. Some coaches identify this as a scramble technique, and others would identify it as a crab block.

LEAD-POST OR POST-AND-DRIVE BLOCK TECHNIQUES

A lead-post or post-and-drive block is the strongest and most effective block in football. The purpose of the lead-post is to move the defender laterally or diagonally, and it is a double-team or power block since it utilizes 2-on-1 blocking. A shoulder-to-shoulder block is also a double-team block. If an opponent is in a defensive gap, it may not be possible to execute the prescribed techniques of a lead-post block, although it might be possible to move him backwards or laterally with shoulder-to-shoulder blocking.

Double-Team Block Techniques

When employing shoulder-to-shoulder double-team blocking, both men step together with the foot nearest the defender and execute the shoulder block techniques described previously, as they adhere to the principles of blocking discussed earlier in this chapter. Each blocker should keep his inside elbow near to his own body so both can execute a shoulder-to-shoulder block together, with the two blockers close together, hip-to-hip, making it difficult for the defender to split them. Diagram 6-13 illustrates the application of these blocking principles, with the offensive right guard and tackle double-teaming the down lineman in the 4-4 defense on the dive play illustrated. The ball carrier breaks for the outside of the double-team block, forcing the scrape-off linebacker to pursue toward the off-tackle hole (left illustration). The guard and tackle merely try to drive their opponent straight back, shoulder-to-shoulder, possibly driving him into the scrape-off linebacker. The dive man reads the near linebacker. If the latter stays inside, the ball carrier continues on his dive course over the outside leg of his offensive tackle (right illustration). If the linebacker moves on-side on the flow of the football, the ball carrier breaks back inside the double-team block over the inside leg of the offensive guard (Diagram 6-13, left illustration).

Lead-Post or Power Block Techniques

Diagram 6-14 illustrates the lead-post or post-and-drive block.
Post Man's Techniques. The post (right tackle) fires out, attempting to drive his face mask into the defender's fold in order to halt the forward charge of his opponent. He exerts pressure upward through the defender's crotch with his helmet in order to destroy the latter's body balance and set up the drive block of his teammate (right end). The post man steps first with his (right) foot nearest the driver. He should attempt to keep his feet, but he may scramble on all fours.

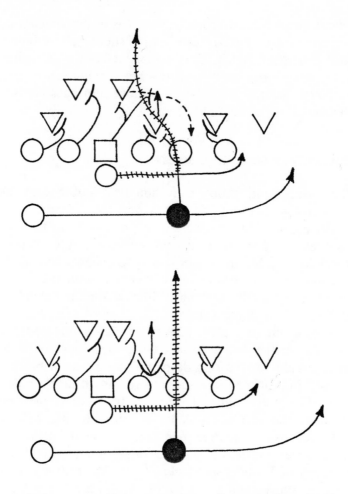

Dive Right - Ball Carrier "Reads" Linebacker

Diagram 6-13
Double-team block techniques (dive right).

However, his legs must be up under his body rather than extended behind it to the rear, or the post man will not be able to blast up through his opponent. While the blocker wants to contact his opponent on the defender's side of the line-of-scrimmage, the post man must be careful he does not knock his opponent backwards, lose contact with his man and make it difficult for the driver to sustain his block and turn him laterally.

Lead Man or Driver's Techniques. The driver (right end) steps with the (left) foot nearest his post man, and executes a straight (left) shoulder block. His target is the defender's near hip. The blocker's head goes behind the defender's body, and he lifts his forearms and elbows into the side of his opponent while pinching with his head. The blocker should drive from the *near* hip *toward* the *far* shoulder of the defender, driving up through his ribs and arm-pit in order to destroy his body balance.

The *post man* swings his tail and hips around toward the driver so that it is not possible for the defender to split the blockers as they move him laterally and diagonally in an effort to widen the hole and, if possible, jam up the pursuit of the interior defenders. The post man (left tackle) must keep pressure on the defender, not giving him an opportunity to fight off the driver and escape from the double-team block.

Coaching Points. The blockers should *not* permit the defender to penetrate the seam. They should combine their forces against the defender and not work against each other. Both blockers must stay on their feet. If the defender goes to the ground, the driver must root him out, widen the hole and smother him.

Diagram 6-14
Lead-post blocking techniques (24 power).

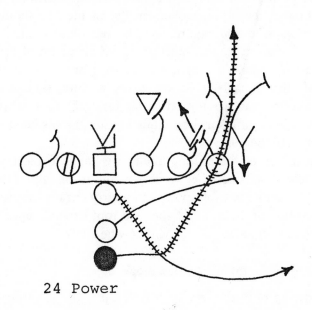

24 Power

TECHNIQUES FOR PULLING LINEMEN

An offensive lineman may pull out of the line in order to trap block, lead interference, seal back to the inside, influence a defender or protect the passer. It is one of the lineman's most important assignments. Excellent guard play in particular is dependent upon exceptionally fine ability to pull out of the offensive line.

Pulling Techniques

The lead-step or pivot-and-step technique, and the cross-step or cross-over technique, are two methods used in pulling a lineman. The advantages of the first method are numerous, and it is used more universally than the cross-over pulling technique. Therefore, the pulling techniques using the lead-step method only will be discussed in detail, and those of the cross-over technique will not be presented.

The Lead-Step Technique. In both techniques, a specific set of directions should be taught rather than just pulling out and running any course. The beginning movement is the basic and most important part of pulling, and for the lead-step or pivot-out technique it may be broken down into the following steps: (1) the snap of the lead arm and (2) the position or direction of the lead step. Although broken into several parts, the initial movement out of the line should be *one complete action or motion,* regardless of the technique used.

From a balanced stance, not tipping off his intent of pulling, the blocker *mentally* puts his weight on his off (far) foot. With the on (near) foot, the offensive blocker takes a direction-and-clearance lead step, pivoting and driving off of his far (off) foot, whipping his far arm across in front of his body, quickly turning his head and body in the direction of the pull.

The near arm of the pulling lineman is snapped back hard, and the near elbow should be as close as possible to his hip. This aids in getting the blocker's body into position to carry out his assignment.

The position of direction of the lead foot depends upon the lineman's offensive assignment, which will now be analyzed.

Techniques for Pulling to Trap Block

Considering *only* the *lead-step* technique, the position or direction of the lead step depends on whether the trap is a short or long one.

The lead-step technique achieves an angle in relationship to the line-of-scrimmage, and since the short trap (Diagrams 6-2 and 6-7) is quicker in that the defender to be blocked is closer to the trapper, the lead-step is at a sharper angle; whereas, the angle and course of the blocker on the long trap (Diagram 6-5) are flatter since the defender is further removed from the trapper. The line-of-direction often is too deep, which puts the trapper in a poor position to execute his running shoulder block; consequently, he takes the improper angle on the lead step, runs an arc and gets too deep on the man he is trapping (not illustrated).

It is important that the weight shifts over the lead step. If it does not, the blocker will raise his body on the second and third steps. This limits his speed and timing in executing his trap block.

Position of Defender to Be Trapped. The next factor to consider is the position of the defender to be trapped. Regardless of whether he has penetrated or has remained in his original position, the emphasis should be on an *inside-out* position on him. If the lead step is taken in the proper direction initially, then the blocker follows the blocking path, thereby obtaining an inside-out position on the defender to be trapped.

Once in the proper running path, the trap block becomes a running shoulder block, with shoulders square, feet wide apart, head up, hit, lift, follow through, keep feet moving after contact, etc., the fundamentals and techniques of which have been discussed already (Diagrams 6-2, 6-5 and 6-7). The trapper must be drilled to drive through his opponent, practically stepping on the latter's toes before executing his driving shoulder block. This insures closeness of contact and proper position on the defender. If the trapper merely tries to block the defender and not drive through him, his power will be dissipated and the play piled up. If he tries to flatten his opponent as he drives through him with a good base, it is not likely the trapper will fall off after contact and lose his opponent. Closeness to the defender's body will insure follow-through by the trapper.

To be proficient in trapping, blockers must be drilled to handle the defender who fires, penetrates, waits in the hole and the one who recognizes the trap and attempts to fill the hole. In the latter case, there is little the trapper can do except try to smother the defender in order to keep the latter from using his arms or legs to trip the ball carrier.

Techniques for Pulling to Lead Interference

When pulling out to lead interference (Diagrams 6-3 and 6-11), the lead step of the pulling lineman is parallel to the line-of-scrimmage for outside plays. However, the depth of the offensive lineman pulling to lead interference will be determined by the type of offensive play, as illustrated in Diagram 6-11 where the on-side (right) guard must pull behind his filling offensive back (fullback). The blocker's pulling course must be such that it will enable him to get to the critical point-of-attack before the ball carrier.

As a pulling lineman turns upfield, he must stay low, dip his inside shoulder, maintain good body balance and control and be ready to block a defender in the hole with a running shoulder block. The defender may be inside with the pulling lineman "sealing" back in order to cut off inside pursuit, or the defender may be to the outside or in the defensive secondary (Diagrams 6-3, 6-11, 6-12 and 6-14). Should the pulling lineman clear the area as he turns upfield without making contact, he should continue to move at top controlled speed until he has the opportunity to block an opponent.

Downfield Blocking Techniques. In blocking downfield, the offensive lineman may employ a running shoulder block, merely attempting to run through the defender or forcing him to change his angle of pursuit on the ball carrier, or the blocker may throw a high, long body block and attempt to cut down the opponent.

Every block executed while running must have maximum controlled speed and aggressiveness. The blocker should not sacrifice body control for speed. In taking short, digging steps, the blocker should continue to run with knees partially flexed, and not permit full extension of the legs, in order to maintain body control. The blocker should keep in mind he is attacking a fighting man, not the position. He should attempt to get into a position where the defender must come through him to get to the ball carrier. Such a position will restrict the defender's area in which to maneuver. The blocker should approach the defender directly and attack him. He should not throw his body wildly into space where he thinks the defender will be positioned, nor should he start his block too far away from the defender. The blocker's contact should be sharp, solid, accurate and with continued effort. Since a body in motion follows the position of the head, the blocker should keep his head up, eyes open and on the target in order to be able to react to the defender's change of position. The target in blocking a man standing in an upright or semi-upright position will be higher than that of the player in a defensive lineman's stance.

Techniques for Pulling to Influence

Although a lineman pulls to influence the defender over him, as illustrated by the right guard in Diagram 6-7, the position or direction of his lead foot depends upon the remainder of his offensive technique. If the offensive lineman who is influencing is trapping short or long, or pulling to the outside as if to lead interference, his lead step achieves a proper angle in relation to the line-of-scrimmage, as was described previously. Of course, the defender one pulling lineman is trying to influence is generally trap blocked by another pulling lineman (Diagram 6-7). All of the techniques for the offensive linemen have been described previously.

In Diagram 6-15 the "influence" principle is the same as that in Diagram 6-7, only the right guard is pulling to influence the defender over his outside shoulder, and the on-side split back (fullback) blocks down on the down (tackle) lineman. All of the other blocking techniques for the offensive linemen have been discussed previously.

Diagram 6-15
Guards pull to influence, back blocks down (48 wham).

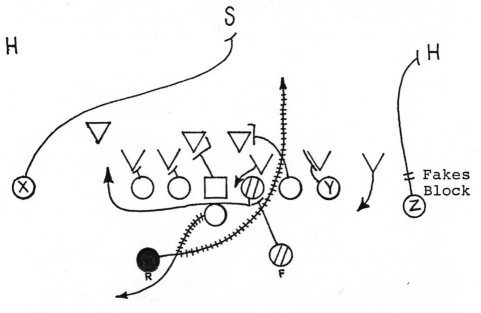

48 Wham

Techniques for Pulling to Cut Off Pursuit

Mention was made previously of pulling an offensive lineman up through the hole to seal back to the inside in order to cut off pursuit. A second category of a lineman sealing off is to pull to cut off backside pŭrsuit, as is illustrated by the off-side (left) tackle and end in Diagram 6-11. These blockers pull down the line with their left guard, just as if they, too, were pulling out of the line. Diagrams 6-13 and 6-14 also illustrate the offensive left tackle cutting off.

The pulling linemen utilize a lead-step technique to pull out of the line, as has been explained previously. They might *legally clip* a defender within the zone specified by the rules, and at times this will be the only way an offensive lineman can keep a defender from pursuing to the football. Otherwise the offensive lineman who is pulling to cut off pursuit employs hook or reach block techniques, which have been explained previously.

Techniques for Pulling to Protect the Passer

Techniques for offensive linemen pulling out of the line to protect the passer are discussed and illustrated in Chapter 8.

SELECTED DRILLS REFERENCE*

(*See* footnote source for 40 football drills which may be used for teaching offensive line fundamentals, skills and techniques.)

---

* Donald E. Fuoss, *Championship Football Drills for Teaching Offensive and Defensive Fundamentals and Techniques* (Englewood Cliffs, N.J.: Prentice-Hall, Inc., 1964), pp. 67-87.

INTRODUCTION

At least half of the success of a pass is dependent upon the player who catches the football. However, there is much more to the passing game for a receiver than just catching the football once it has been thrown within his reach. Other very important factors include releasing from the line-of-scrimmage, executing the exact route called, using proper faking techniques, learning the value of good position when competing for the football with a defender and carrying the ball once the reception has been made. Therefore, pass receiving techniques will be categorized and discussed as releasing, maneuvering, catching and running techniques, after first considering requisites of end play personnel.

Requisites of End Play Personnel

The responsibilities of the offensive end are increasing constantly with the complicated offenses of today. The *tight end* must be a good blocker if the running attack is to be successful. If his pass catching skills are limited, then a team's offensive passing attack involving the tight end in pass patterns is minimal. Therefore, if possible, the tight end should be one of your better athletes, and he should possess quickness, agility and good hands or pass catching skills, along with being a hard-nosed football player who is capable of making the running at-

Coaching Offensive Tight End– Flanker Fundamentals, Skills and Techniques

tack effective when his blocking skills must be utilized.

The *split end* or flanker must be a fine athlete, too, although speed, the quickness to get open and the ability to catch the football, are more important than physical size and being hard-nosed. The split end's blocking is generally limited to crack-back and downfield blocking, and frequently when a two-tight-end offense is employed, the typical split end is replaced by another tight end. In many instances, the split end and flanker back positions are interchangeable.

OFFENSIVE END STANCE

The *tight end* may assume a more comfortable, elongated, staggered stance than that of the interior lineman (Chapter 6). However, the tight end must assume a good fundamental, balanced stance since the successful execution of his blocking and quick release from the line-of-scrimmage depends upon it.

The advantages of a three-point stance for your *wide flankers* (X and Z) are as follows: it eliminates leaning or moving, there is less chance of being held up at the line-of-scrimmage and it permits a quicker release across the line-of-scrimmage and into the defensive secondary.

If you flip-flop your wide receivers, it is likely you will have to teach them both a right- and left-handed stance. By always aligning with the inside foot forward, the number of steps run in a specific pattern remains constant if the receiver is on the right or left side.

In Chapter 8, the pass blocking techniques, and screen and draw blocking techniques, will be presented for the offensive linemen.

RELEASING TECHNIQUES

A successful passing attack depends, in no small degree, upon the ability of the offensive ends to get free at the line-of-scrimmage and into the open to receive the pass. If they fail to get out into the pass pattern quickly, their speed and ability are of little value. When a receiver permits himself to be held up, it becomes almost impossible to complete the pass to him. In order to have good timing on a pass, the receivers must get past the line-of-scrimmage quickly.

There is a tendency to jam the receivers at the line-of-scrimmage in certain situations. Ends should be drilled to expect this. Seldom will they be permitted to release into the defensive secondary un-molested in a passing situation. Therefore, the receivers should be coached and drilled to release quickly and get away fast without being detained. The receivers should be taught several different releasing techniques so they will not become confused and expend valuable time and effort getting out on a pass.

There are a number of different releasing techniques, some more complicated than others. The simpler the technique the better, if it is effective in aiding the receiver in releasing. Two or three techniques will be sufficient, if they are effectively performed. Several techniques are as follows: straight outside release; split out; quick head-and-shoulder fake in one direction, go the other way; fake block or con-trolled block and slide out; crawl out on all fours. There are others, but the above will suffice for illustrative purposes.

Outside Release and Splitting Out Techniques

The simplest and probably the most effective release is the straight outside release, wherein the receiver merely sprints through the outside hip of the defender over him and slams him with his inside forearm, in order to get loose from the defender and get into his pass route.

Receiving ends should always release outside the defensive tackle and inside the defensive end, when it is possible to do so. In other than an obvious passing situation, the end who is employing a tight release may be more effective and deceptive than one who is releasing from a flanked position. In the former, if the end will merely move out an extra yard from his regular position, he can exert additional pressure on a defensive lineman and/or linebacker. He will also have more room to clear the line-of-scrimmage.

Split Rules for Flankers. The splits of the wide receivers (X and Z) are determined by the horizontal placement of the football and the receiver's specific assignment on a given play. In Diagram 7-1 (top illustration), if the ball is in the middle of the field, the flankers will split the distance between the hash marks and sidelines. In Diagram 7-1 (bottom illustration), if the ball is on the hash mark, the receiver into the sideline (Z or X) aligns himself no closer than 4 yards to that sideline; the receiver (X or Z) to the wide side of the field aligns himself 2 yards on either side of the opposite hash mark.

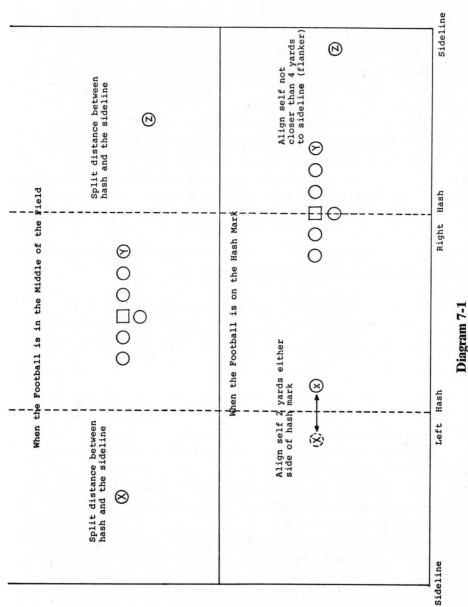

Diagram 7-1

Split rules for flankers, depending on horizontal placement of football.

From these basic split rules for the wide flankers, the individual receiver adjusts to best enable him to carry out his particular assignment on a given play. As an illustration, versus a 4-deep secondary, a wide split will probably force the opposition to cover or fill from an invert zone or 1-on-1 coverage, rather than from a corner rotation. Conversely, a split of only 6–7 yards versus a 4-deep secondary would permit corner coverage and rotation, and the secondary would not have to employ an invert. On the other hand, the flanker might wish to split only 6–7 yards in order to crack-back block effectively. Versus a 3-deep secondary, by taking a wide split the flanker can stretch the zone and force 1-on-1 coverage. Therefore, your flankers should be taught how their splits affect the coverage they will receive and the bearing it has on the play being run.

Head-and-Shoulder Fake Techniques

The receivers should be taught to execute a quick head-and-shoulder fake inside, then slide outside and vice versa. They should be drilled to stay low and move quickly, because defensive men will instinctively bump the pass receivers if they are high and slow in releasing downfield.

When employing the head-and-shoulder fake, the receiver should over-emphasize his actions or the defensive player will not be fooled. The receiver should take a quick jab step to the inside staying in a low position, swing his head and shoulders hard and fast to the inside and then push off quickly with his inside foot to the outside. The procedure is reversed if he wishes to release inside. He should fake outside first and then drive back inside.

Fake Block or Controlled Block Techniques

A simple technique for the tight end is to take a quick jab step with his lead foot, snap his head back and bring his hands and arms upward hard and fast as if he is going to execute a high pass block on the defensive player. Instinctively, the defensive man will rise up or step back so that he is not struck in the face. The hesitancy of the defensive player is all the offensive end needs to slide out unmolested.

A second technique is to drive into the defender low and hard while executing a controlled shoulder block, release and slide off into the pattern. It must be an aggressive block or the defensive player will not be fooled. Generally, under these circumstances, a properly trained defensive player will release the offensive end as he reacts to the block.

Crawl Out Techniques

An offensive end may shoot outside the defensive player by scrambling on his hands and feet for a couple of yards, and then getting up and going quickly when he gets past the defensive player. He may wish to use a head-and-shoulder fake first and then crawl out on all fours. It may be necessary to block out aggressively and then crawl out.

When two players are trying to pinch the end, he may dive on all fours between them and then come up running. Of course if they hold him after he makes his move, defensive holding should be called by the officials.

Some coaches teach a pivot-out or roll-off technique, which is not as basic and common as the previously mentioned techniques. Nor is it the simplest technique for the high school athlete to perform, since he must be careful he does not get his feet crossed and tied up at the line-of-scrimmage.

If two defenders are pinching the offensive end, it may be better to block one and release from him, rather than try to fight both defenders. Or the end may wish to employ the crawl-out technique, going between both of the defenders.

Sometimes a receiver will have to use a combination of releasing techniques to get into the defensive secondary. He may employ a fake block or controlled block technique to release from the defensive lineman, and use a quick head-and-shoulder fake to get by the linebacker.

Many defenders are taught to play the head of the offensive man. Therefore, a quick head fake technique may be sufficient for the receiver to get out. If two players move into position to hold up the receiver, he can expect to be jammed from both the inside and outside. Therefore, the receiver will probably have to utilize a combination of releasing techniques to get off the line-of-scrimmage.

As soon as the release is made and the intended receiver is beyond the first defensive man, he must get his body under complete control as soon as possible. He should then run his route, using maneuvering techniques to get open.

MANEUVERING TECHNIQUES

Unless the quick pass is being thrown, the receiver has very little opportunity to run a straight course to a pre-determined spot without being detected and countered by the defense. A well-drilled defensive player will react and counter immediately as soon as the receiver releases from the line-of-scrimmage. It is for this reason that the receivers must be cognizant of the tactical situation, including the yardage necessary for a first down.

Controlled Use of the Body

Maneuvering is controlled use of the body. The eyes, arms and legs, and directional movement and speed, play an important part in the total effort to confuse the opposition. In order to deceive the defender and create a favorable situation in which to catch the football, the receiver must utilize his assets and exploit any defensive weakness that is available. As an illustration, he wants the defender to think he is going to run a deep route, when the receiver actually is going to run a short one, or vice versa. This can be done by faking his speed or using a head-and-shoulder fake. When running the route and faking, speed is not always important. A deliberate fake and then *quickness* is more acceptable than a fast, hurried fake. After the fake is complete and the final break for the ball is in progress, the receiver should make his move at full speed, but under good body control.

Upon releasing from the line, the receiver immediately obtains eye contact with the defensive player assigned to protect the zone or area in which the ball is to be thrown. The coverage may be zone, man-for-man or a combination, and the receiver will gain an immediate advantage if he can recognize the type of coverage. He should try to observe the initial reaction of the defenders at the start of the play. They may not recognize *Pass* immediately. Then certain areas of the defensive secondary will immediately open up for the receiver. He should quickly recognize this advantage and exploit it immediately by going into the exposed area. In all probability, he can then look for the football to be thrown much sooner than originally anticipated when this situation occurs.

To the contrary, the receiver must be careful that he does not tip off the fact that a pass is going to be thrown. When this occurs, the defenders gain the advantage.

Receiver Versus Defender

Despite the fact that the defender may be taught to play the football and not the receiver, it becomes a personal battle between the two opposing players. As an illustration, the defender must not permit the receiver to get behind him and he must keep the receiver in front of him and watch the point of the football. Therefore, the receiver only has to indicate a determined effort to get behind the defender, which results in the former gaining all of the territory in front of the defender in which to catch the football. Consequently, a good receiver is a good actor, and he will create a false impression, tending to confuse the defender. He then makes it easier to deceive him and get open in order to catch the football.

The importance of speed cannot be minimized, despite previous remarks to the apparent contrary. Speed is probably the most important single factor which contributes to the success of the pass receiver. Most pass routes are run by starting fast, easing up to execute deceptive maneuvers and finishing with a burst of speed in an effort to get to and catch the football. In order to compete on an equal basis with the defenders, a receiver must constantly work on a quick start, change-of-pace, change of direction and a tremendous finish. Therefore, the speed of a receiver is certainly a deciding factor in the completion of the forward pass. In the final analysis, however, the receiver still must be able to catch the football. Consequently, good judgment and good timing on the part of the receiver are actually more essential than exceptional speed and the ability to fake. The receiver must have a good pair of hands and be able to catch the ball, or it is a "no yardage gained" play if he does not make the reception.

Faking Techniques to "Beat" Defenders

A good receiver learns to keep his body between the opposition and the ball. There are a number of ways of doing this, such as through speed, quickness, agility, maneuverability and the use of his hips and shoulders. There are other ways of beating the defender, such as by employing the following techniques:

1. Fake in one direction with the head and shoulders and break in the opposite direction.

2. Fake running deep, then hook in front of the defender. The receiver explodes fast as though going deep, stops quickly (at a specified depth) with one foot in front of the other, pivots on the outside foot and comes (hooks) back inside toward the passer.

3. Fake running deep, then hook and slide. The maneuver is the same as above, only the receiver slides away from the defender as the latter moves forward to cover him.

4. Hook and go. The receiver executes a hook, forcing the defender to come up fast to play him. Then the receiver rolls around the defender and breaks behind him for the pass.

5. Square-out (in) cut. Run and then stop with feet parallel. Lower the tail. Drive and pivot off of the inside foot (if running the out).

There are numerous other techniques, as shown in Diagram 7-2, a *Passing Tree,* illustrating the individual routes or cuts for X, Y and Z. Note that X and Z as wide flankers both run the same individual routes. Zone 1 indicates the *short* pass routes; zone 2 the *medium* routes and zone 3 the *deep* routes. No effort will be made to illustrate coordinated pass patterns, although several will be included in Chapter 8.

The receiver has a designated area to perform his fake, which may be used as an aiming point. He is also limited in the amount of time he has to get open. A shoulder fake may be all the receiver needs to get open. Often he will have to use speed and maneuverability in order to get open. He should not worry about complicated footwork. He has freedom in running his route, although the defender may harass him. After the ball is in the air, the defender cannot molest him. As the receiver makes his break to get open, he should look for the ball. After turning to look at the ball, the receiver should *never* be conscious of the defenders in his area. His objective now is to get to the ball and catch it. Worrying about the defender leads to interception, as the defender's objective is either to keep the receiver from catching the football or intercept the pass.

Be a Good Decoy

In order for pass patterns to be effective and to free a receiver, all receivers should be good decoys. In many pass patterns, there is a designated receiver and then alternates. A player cannot make a concerted effort to get open only when he is the designated receiver or the first alternate, and slough off and give less than his best effort

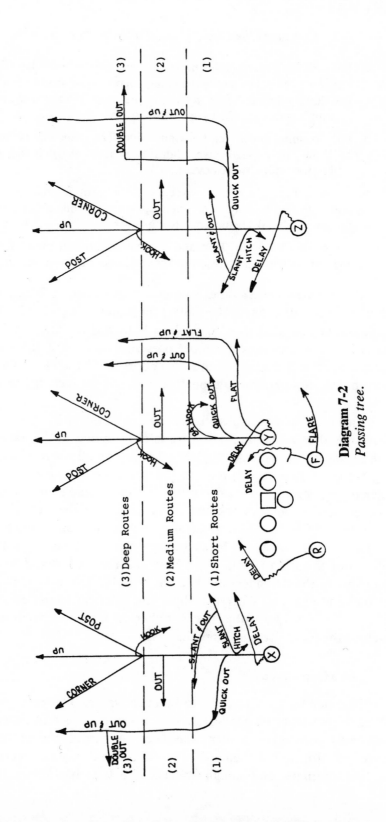

Diagram 7-2
Passing tree.

when he is the second or third alternate receiver. Should the latter occur, certain phases of the pass offense will be ineffective. Then the passing team has relinquished an advantage it may hold over the opposition, which it could exploit if all receivers were good decoys.

Diagram 7-3 illustrates a dozen *twin flanker* patterns with Z flanked outside of X. For simplicity purposes, the name or terminology tells X (the inside receiver) which pattern to run and Z learns his individual (companion) patterns. When R is called into the pattern as R-Up, X learns which pattern (*Flat*) complements the R-Up pattern. If the fullback is called into the pattern, *FB Flare,* then X and Z run their slant patterns. The only exception is Z *Delay,* where X runs a flat pattern, with Z delaying and then crossing behind him.

If sprint-out pass action is employed, the blocking is simply back-side protection for the off-side of the line, unless Y is called into the pattern (such as Y Delay), with the on-side blocking 1 and 2 and the R back blocking 3, unless called into the pattern. If the latter occurs, the FB blocks 3, otherwise 4 (unless 4 drops, then the FB helps on 3).

By Z lining up 3–4 yards away from X, these combination patterns force special coverages, other than merely man-on-man.

CATCHING TECHNIQUES

Catching the football is an art which combines timing, body control and excellent hands. The average receiver can make the easy catch. The good receiver makes the difficult catch. Catching a football with harassment at the time of the catch is slightly more of a problem than the difficulties encountered before and after the reception. The receiver is vulnerable to being "clobbered" when he handles the high pass, which requires a jumping catch. His hands are above his head and his feet are off the ground as the defenders converge and attempt to separate him from the football. Poor receivers hear *footsteps* and are not able to catch the football *in trouble.*

Some receivers often concentrate more on maneuvering and evading the defenders than on catching the football, and do not run the prescribed patterns or routes. With the exception of the quarterback, the pass receiver is faced with more problems of timing and detail than any other member of the team.

The receiver should always expect the ball to be poorly thrown,

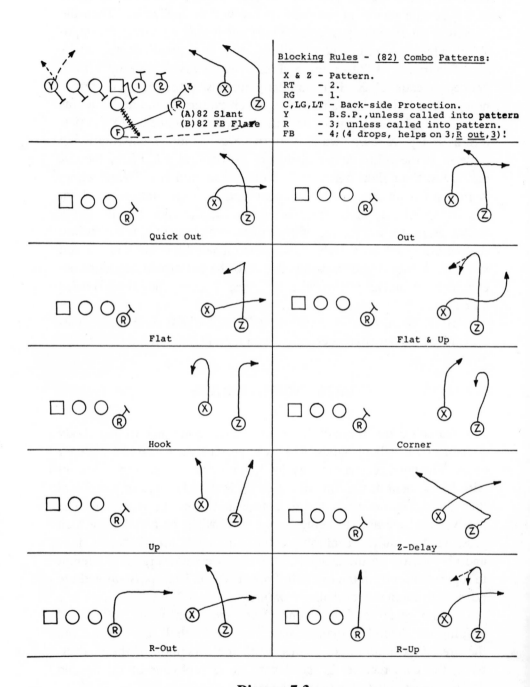

Diagram 7-3
(82) combination pass patterns and blocking rules.

then he will never be surprised when he gets a poorly thrown pass. Since the quarterback may have to throw the ball sooner than originally planned, the receiver should be prepared to make the reception at all times. He should run his route deep enough for a first down or a touchdown, but the receiver should not expect to score on every reception.

Look the Ball into the Hands

A forward pass is successful only if the receiver gains possession of the ball. The prime consideration should be concentration, and the receiver should *look the football into his hands*. He should concentrate only on catching the ball first, before attempting to run with it. If a receiver does not master this fundamental, he will never become a good receiver.

Do Not Fight the Ball

Do not try to catch the ball until it is ready to be caught, is the second fundamental. Do not fight the ball, stay relaxed, is another principle. Always try to catch the ball with the hands. They should be loose, soft, pliable and flexible. It has been said that good pass reception starts and ends in the player's hands. Keeping the hands loose makes it possible for the receiver to adjust to the speed and direction of the ball as he moves to catch it. As the ball makes contact with the receiver's hands, there should be a slight give in the arms to cushion the impact. The receiver should run with his hands about chest high, swinging his arms naturally in order to aid him with his running. By carrying his arms in this position, he can reach quickly, and at the last instant, to catch the football.

Gain Control of the Ball Immediately

To be able to catch the ball and hold on to it while being tackled simultaneously is the mark of a good receiver. Therefore, another fundamental of pass reception is to gain control of the football immediately.

Placement of Fingers, Thumbs and Hands

Footwork is important, as is being in a good balanced position with the body under control, in order to jump, stop or cut at any given moment without wasting time. While the position of the fingers, thumbs and hands are important in making the reception, sometimes coaches tend to over-emphasize these fundamentals. A receiver should be permitted to catch the football in the easiest and most natural way. If the receiver has sufficient drill and is able to make the reception, whatever way he does it is probably natural to him. However, the following additional reception techniques are suggested:

1. If facing the passer and the ball is thrown at or below the waist, the catch should be made with the thumbs turned *outward* and palms facing upward.
2. If facing the passer and the ball is thrown chest high or higher, the catch should be made with the thumbs turned *inward* and the palms away from the face.
3. In making the catch going away from the passer, the receiver's palms should be open toward his face and his thumbs should be turned *outward*.

An effort should be made to catch the football on the fingertips. When caught with the palms, there is not sufficient cushion to make the catch easy. The football should be caught away from the body in order to eliminate the possibility of it striking the pads or body and making the catch difficult. While it is not always possible to catch the football with two hands, a good receiver can tip the ball at times and make a one-handed catch. A one-handed stab will often result in a deflected ball that is likely to be intercepted. A receiver should remember the concluding coaching point, "If you cannot catch the football, be certain your opponent does not catch it." Desire is the first requisite of a good receiver, and a receiver can improve his pass catching skills by repetitive practice.

RUNNING TECHNIQUES

After catching the football, the receiver becomes a runner. However, many passes are dropped because the receiver tries to run with the ball before having possession of it securely, or before putting it away. Therefore, the first principle or coaching point is to admonish your receivers to "put the ball away every time" upon catching it, so this will become second nature to the receivers.

You should coach the receiver to *turn upfield immediately*, running as swiftly as he can, directly toward the opposition's goal line.

A cause of fumbling is when the receiver (ball carrier) starts cutting back laterally or diagonally across the field and is tackled by pursuers from the *blind* side. Seldom is he set for the tackle, which is generally very aggressive, since the ball carrier seldom sees the tacklers, and this is in effect like being *clotheslined*. If the receiver does not fumble the football, he is likely either to lose yardage or must certainly minimize the yardage gained by running laterally or diagonally to the line-of-scrimmage. Therefore, upon catching the football, stress the importance of the receiver heading upfield directly toward the opposition's goal line.

Your receivers should practice some of the same running techniques as the backs; namely, straight arm, shoulder drive and possibly a cross-over or side-step technique. Since the receivers must master cutting techniques when maneuvering in order to get open, this may be all the receiver needs in the way of running techniques. However, it would be wise to teach your receivers (ball carriers) to run in a *hitting* position so their vulnerable area is protected. The body should be flexed slightly at the waist, exposing only a hard-shell surface of shoulder pads, helmet, elbows and knees to the tackler, so that the ball carrier is able to deliver a blow to the tackler instead of being vulnerable to a smashing tackle. Uncoiling from a hitting position, plus the determination not to be tackled, is the only technique a receiver (ball carrier) will be able to use and all that he will need on occasion.

SELECTED DRILLS REFERENCE*

(*See* footnote source for 47 football drills for teaching passing and receiving fundamentals, skills and techniques.)

---

* Donald E. Fuoss, *Championship Football Drills for Teaching Offensive and Defensive Fundamentals and Techniques* (Englewood Cliffs, N.J.: Prentice-Hall, Inc., 1964), pp. 131-146.

INTRODUCTION

Pass protection skills are probably the most difficult and demanding ones offensive linemen must perform in modern-day football. An offensive lineman's problem is compounded further not only by jumping alignments, stunting defenses, dogging linebackers and safety blitzes, but also by defensive pass rush techniques (Chapter 11) which have become exacting and refined, too.

Time Factors for Pass Protection

The length of time the offensive linemen must sustain their blocks to provide adequate pass protection depends on such factors as: (1) the depth from where the passer sets up and releases the football; (2) the distance the football is thrown to the receiver; (3) the side of the line where the linemen are positioned in relation to the receiver.

The type of pass thrown will determine where the passer will set up. On a quick pass, the passer is likely to set up at 1–3 yards. On most pocket passes he sets up at 6–8 yards from the line-of-scrimmage, and then works up into his pocket of protection. Therefore, offensive linemen must have a conception of the type of pass which is being thrown and the depth at which the quarterback sets up, so they know which pass protection tech-

Coaching Offensive Line Passing Game Fundamentals, Skills and Techniques

niques they must employ. If their passer is throwing the quick pass from 1–3 yards depth from the line-of-scrimmage, the offensive linemen will not employ the same pass protection techniques as when the quarterback sets up at 7 yards.

Minimum "Time" Needed by the Passer. Then, too, the offensive linemen must have a conception of "time" in order to protect their passer adequately. A passer should be able to throw almost any pass, if he has protection for 4.5 seconds (from the time the quarterback receives the center's snap until he releases the football). This is based on the assumption that the quarterback is able to set up at 7 yards in approximately 1.3 seconds. However, for the quarterback to concentrate solely on *reading* the coverage and getting the football to the open receiver, he must have a minimum of 3.5 seconds. It is very important that he be *confident* that his blockers will protect him for at least this length of time.

POCKET PROTECTION BLOCKING TECHNIQUES

Although there is a difference of opinion among coaches as to the *best* pass protection techniques for pocket or drop-back passes, which will be noted, all coaches agree the primary objective is to form a pocket around the passer, and keep the rushers out of *no man's land*. Therefore, the first requisite of a good pass protector is the desire to pass block and get the job done!

Various Blocking Schemes for Pocket or Drop-Back Passing

Offensive linemen can protect their passer in several ways. One such method is the conventional cup protection technique, with all of the protectors zoning or area blocking, and no one is assigned to a particular rusher until the opponent enters an offensive blocker's zone or area. Another method is *man* blocking, where each offensive blocker is assigned a specific defender. If the latter comes as a rusher, the blocker has him all the way. If the opponent does not rush, the offensive lineman is "free" to help out as a blocker where needed in his immediate area. If the blocker is an offensive back and his specific defender (usually a linebacker) does not rush (dog) after first "check" blocking for the rush, the offensive back then releases into the pattern as an outlet (safety valve) receiver. Another method of pass protection is a combination of the first two methods, in that two offensive linemen (or a lineman and a back) are responsible for two rushers, generally a stacked tandem of a down lineman and a linebacker. The two offensive players responsible for the two defenders will not utilize cup protection in the same sense as in the first method, nor are they assigned a specific rusher as in the second method of pass protection. Each *man* blocks the defender who charges (or fires) into his respective area. All three methods of pass protection will be illustrated.

Open Formations, Two to Five Receivers. In present-day football, one method of pass protection is not adequate. Most offensive-minded football coaches consistently employ open formations with wide receivers flanked to both sides or twin flankers (Diagram 7-3) to the same side. Therefore, on most passes at least two receivers release, with the tight end either being called into a particular pattern, or he may have to *read* the rush or blitz and remain in as an added protector. Also, he may release regardless of the rush or blitz if he is the *hot* receiver. Either or both offensive backs may release, too, so that on occasion the offensive team has five-man pass patterns, with only the five interior linemen as personal protectors for their quarterback. Or from the conventional open formations with only the two wide receivers releasing, eight offensive blockers are available to protect the passer. All types of blocking will be illustrated.

A "Hot" System. Pass-minded coaches have devised a *hot* system to handle the rush or blitz. The *hot* receiver is either the tight end (Y) or one of the offensive backs, who *reads* a defender (usually a linebacker) and *"eye balls"* him. Should the latter fire, both the quarterback and the *hot* receiver are reading his tough rush, and the passer dumps the football to his *hot* receiver, who looks for it as soon as he clears the line-of-scrimmage.

Conversely, the defense may counter by sending eight rushers and attempting to handle the *hot* receiver by going 3-deep *man* coverage (versus Y) in the defensive secondary. Therefore, when Y is the *hot* receiver, both he and his quarterback must be taught to read both the 3-deep *zone* and *man* secondary coverage. If it is the latter, the quarterback will probably attempt to pass to one of his wide receivers (X or Z), who will be working 1-on-1 versus single defenders in *man* coverage. If one of the offensive backs is designated as *hot,* he may release regardless of the blitz and the quarterback looks for his back as his *hot* receiver, dumping the football to him. Therefore, in order to have a successful passing attack in present-day football, a team must devise and utilize a *hot* system to handle the defensive rushes and blitzes.

Ratio of Protectors to Rushers. When the ratio of pass rushers to blockers is either even (7–7 or 8–8) or favors the offensive team (eight blockers to seven or less rushers), assuming there is not an individual breakdown in a blocker's pass protection, the passer should be able to "read" the coverage and get the football to the open receiver. However, when the ratio of rushers is greater than the number of blockers who are assigned to protect their passer, then the latter must either dump the football to his *hot* receiver or throw quickly to one of his wide flankers, if he reads 3-deep zone coverage with eight rushers coming on a blitz.

Zone or Area Cup Protection. Diagram 8-1 illustrates zone or area cup protection versus both (Oklahoma 5-2) linebackers dogging to the strong side. Diagram 8-2 illustrates the same stunt, plus the free safety blitzing, with the defensive secondary rotating into a 3-deep zone. However, the defensive "*look*" is different in the two diagrams

Diagram 8-1
Zone or area cup protection versus strong-side rush (double dog)–Oklahoma 5-2 defense.

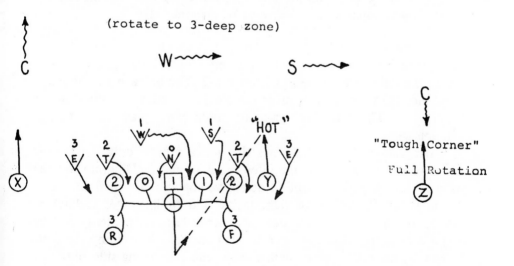

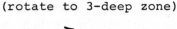

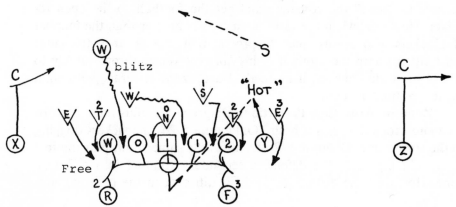

Diagram 8-2

Zone or area cup protection versus safety blitz (strong-side rush, weak safety blitz)–Oklahoma 5-2 defense.

for the offensive left tackle and the split back (R) to the weak side. The left tackle must area block the safety who is blitzing, and R area blocks the defensive tackle in Diagram 8-2. The defensive right end is *free*, since the rushers outnumber the blockers, and Y is utilized as the *hot* receiver. The defensive secondary could easily play *man* coverage with this stunt.

Diagram 8-3 also illustrates the above points, only the double dog is to the weak side of the offensive line, and in Diagram 8-4 the strong safety is blitzing (not all defensive coaches flop their safeties). In the latter, the offensive right tackle and fullback get a different *"look."* In Diagram 8-4 the defensive secondary undoubtedly will be in a 3-deep *zone*, which will permit the quarterback to dump the football to Y, his *hot* receiver, when they read the strong-side blitz. Or another alternative is to teach Y to stay in when he reads this blitz, offering maximum protection (8–8), and the passer throws to X or Z. Then the right tackle would block the blitzing safety coming into his

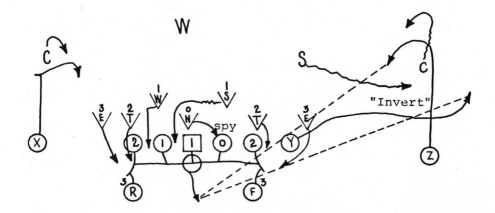

Diagram 8-3

Zone or area cup protection versus weak-side rush (double dog)–Oklahoma 5-2 defense.

zone; Y would block the defensive tackle and the fullback would area or zone block the defensive end.

Note in Diagram 8-2 versus the free (weak) safety blitz that Y releases anyway, even if the strong safety moves over Y and plays him *man* coverage, because Y does not aid in protecting his passer by remaining in. In Diagram 8-4, Y could aid in the protection, as indicated, if he were trained and drilled to do so.

Utilizing the Safety Blitz, and Blocking It. Three observations are pertinent to utilizing the safety blitz and blocking it: (1) most defensive teams will rotate to a 3-deep *zone,* because it is safer than playing 3-deep *man* coverage; (2) using the safety blitz consistently is a calculated risk, especially with *man* coverage; (3) an offensive team must get plenty of practice blocking the blitz (and all defensive schemes and stunts). If you *burn* the defense, especially when a receiver beats a single defender 1-on-1, generally the opposition will stop blitzing.

The numbers assigned to the defensive players and the offensive linemen and backs in Diagrams 8-1 to 8-4 are used merely to signify whom the blockers pick up when the rushers come into their area, despite the fact that area or zone blocking is being utilized in providing cup protection for the passer. If the offensive center, as an illustration, were to go after the man on his nose, and the defense was stunting as in Diagrams 8-1 to 8-4, there would be a void in the cup

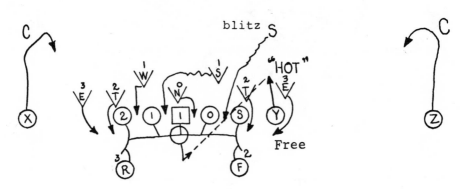

Diagram 8-4

Zone or area cup protection versus safety blitz (weak-side rush, strong safety blitz)—Oklahoma 5-2 defense.

protection, and a linebacker coming off of the nose-man's tail on his stunt would come through clean with no one blocking him. Conversely, if the nose-guard plays straight up, hitting and reacting to the play, the center must be drilled to read this, too, and zone block the rusher.

"Man" Pass Protection. Diagram 8-5 illustrates *man* pass blocking, where each offensive lineman and the split backs are individually assigned a specific man to block. Y is utilized as a *hot* receiver. He can force the defensive end and outside linebacker to make a defensive adjustment (Diagram 8-5), by splitting out a yard or so wider from his normal spacing, which will put the defensive end in close proximity to the offensive right tackle, who will block him, and will reduce the rush of the outside *contain* (OLB) man. After check blocking, the fullback will release in the strong-side flat or inside on a pattern if the OLB does not rush. If the end remains outside, and the linebacker inside and they come on a tough rush, this can be blocked without difficulty, although the quarterback can dump the ball to Y as soon as both read the strong-side linebacker dogging (firing).

Diagram 8-5
Man protection versus strong-side rush–pro 4-3 defense.

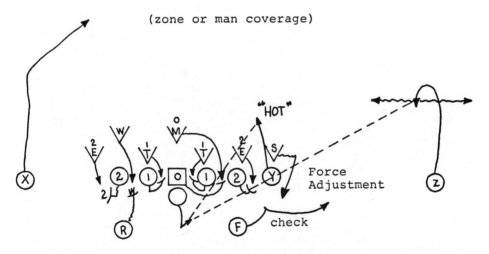

Linemen block linemen; backs block linebackers

Note in *man* blocking, the offensive center has the middle linebacker (O) all the way if he fires, as compared to his zone or area assignment in Diagrams 8-1 to 8-4. However, if the offensive linemen were *man* blocking the Oklahoma 5-2, the center would take *O* on his stunt, the guards *1* and the tackles *2*, all the way. (The blocking principle would be the same as illustrated in Diagram 8-5.)

Diagram 8-6 illustrates the application of turn-out pass protection blocking rules. The fullback picks up the *plugger,* who dogs late after the offensive right guard turns out on the defensive tackle. Versus the eagle adjustment to the split end's side, *R* check blocks the linebacker and then releases into the pattern since the *plugger* does not rush.

Diagram 8-6
Man protection (turn-out blocking) versus Oklahoma 5-2 defense.

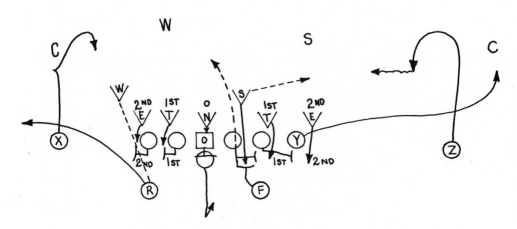

```
Turn-Out Blocking Rules:
C     - 0.
Gs    - 1st man on line.
Ts    - 2nd man on line.
Backs - Pluggers (LBers); none, release.
```

Diagram 8-7 illustrates the application of the same *man* turn-out blocking rules versus the pro 4-3 defense, with the adjustment to the back side, and *R* picking up the weak linebacker on his rush. Since the strong linebacker does not rush, the fullback check blocks first, then releases.

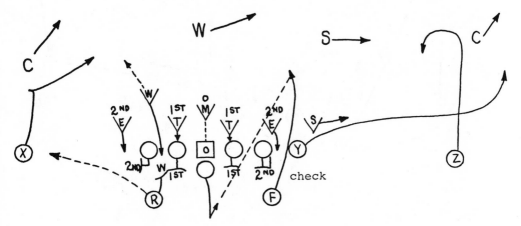

Turn-Out Blocking Rules: (Same as Diagram 8-6)

Diagram 8-7

Man protection (turn-out blocking) versus pro 4-3, split adjustment.

Diagram 8-8 illustrates the application of *man* (not turn-out) rule blocking versus the pro 4-3 *over* (odd) defensive alignment. It could be zone or area blocked, too, since the ratio of blockers to rushers is even (7–7). Diagram 8-8 also illustrates utilizing the offensive fullback as the *hot* receiver, with Y taking a wider split than normal, forcing the defensive end and strong-side linebacker to exchange positions.

Combination Pass Protection. Diagram 8-9 illustrates a combination of area and man blocking principles versus the 4-3 stack, which could be zone or area blocked, too, since the rushers-blockers ratio is even (7–7).

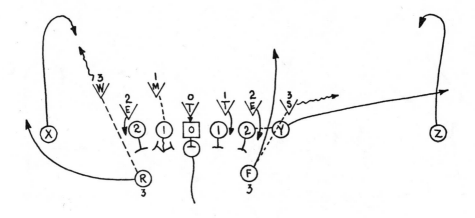

Diagram 8-8
Man protection versus pro 4-3 over (odd) defense.

Blocking the Split 6 or 4-4 for Drop-Back Passing

The Split 6 or 4-4 defensive alignment presents a different problem than any of those cited previously, in that eight defenders are either on or near the line-of-scrimmage. Should the opposition rush all eight men, seven blockers could not adequately protect the passer. Therefore, few teams try to area or zone block the 4-4 alignment. While most teams which play this as a regular defense seldom come with all eight rushers, a method or scheme must be provided for blocking them when all eight defenders do rush.

Automatic to Maximum Protection Until Tendencies Are Established. From the scouting report and through the breakdown and study of game films (at the college level in particular), the offensive team will have charted the defensive tendencies of their Split 6 opponent, including the different stunts, with which coverages and in which down-distance situations. This analytical-frequency breakdown will be the starting point for blocking the defensive alignment stunts, and

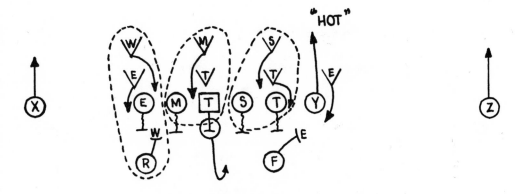

```
Blocking Scheme,
Combo Protection:
LT-R block E-WLB
LG-C block N(T)-MLB
RG-T block T-SLB
FB    block E
```

Diagram 8-9

Combination pass protection versus 4-3 stack defense.

will include not only the type of protection which will be utilized, but the type of passes and number of receivers in the routes, too. The game plan will be fashioned in this manner.

Until the offensive team can verify the reliability-validity of their previously analyzed tendencies, and/or until they can secure new defensive tendencies on their Split 6 opponent, the offense will have to *automatic* to maximum (8 versus 8) protection (when throwing straight drop-back passes from the pocket) and release only two wide receivers (Diagram 8-10). The quarterback keys the defensive safety man, and throws to either X or Z working 1-on-1 versus a single defender, away from the side the safety man favors or plays initially.

A better blocking scheme is for Y to read the linebacker over him, and should the latter drop instead of firing, then Y goes out into the pattern. If the linebacker fires, then Y will block him. Diagram 8-11 illustrates the same blocking scheme as in Diagram 8-10, except the strong-side tackle uses turn-out blocking on the defensive end, and

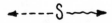

(QB keys safety; throws to
opposite side safety favors)

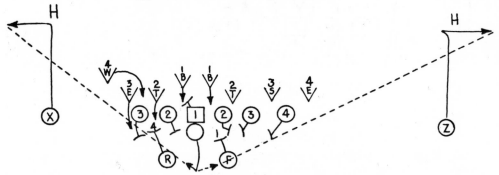

Maximum protection - 8 blockers versus 8 rushers

Diagram 8-10
Man protection versus split 6 or 4-4 defense.

Y reads his linebacker and reacts as indicated above. In Diagram 8-10 should the linebacker drop off, then the right tackle would *not* have a specific man to block but Y would still block the defensive end. Therefore Diagram 8-11 illustrates a better blocking scheme.

Diagram 8-12 illustrates man and combination pass protection, with Y reading his linebacker the same as explained previously (Diagram 8-11).

Diagram 8-13 is still another blocking scheme, where Y releases immediately as the hot receiver. The strong side of the formation has four blockers versus four rushers, but the weak side has only three blockers versus four rushers, should all eight rushers come. In this situation, the quarterback must get rid of the football immediately. The center reads the front inside linebacker first and blocks him if he fires. If he does not fire, but the back-side linebacker comes, the center drops and tries to pick him up. R reads the inside linebacker to his side first. If he fires, R gets set to take him. He may or may not get help from his center. If the inside linebacker does not come, R turns

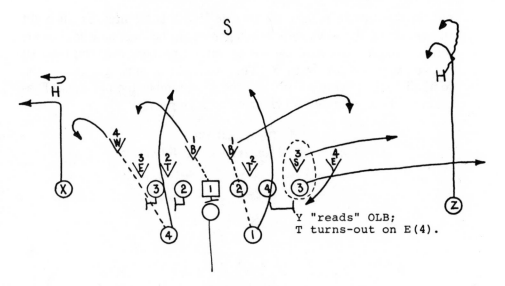

Diagram 8-11
Man protection versus split 6 or 4-4 defense.

Diagram 8-12
Man and combination pass protection versus split 6 or 4-4 defense.

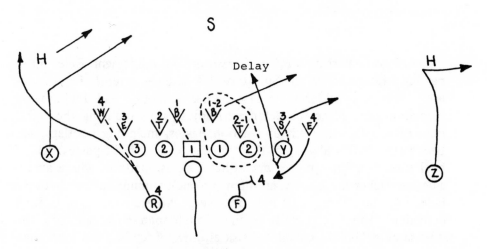

```
Blocking Scheme:
RG-RT Combo block T-ILB
Others block "man"
Y "read" OLB
```

out on the outside backer to his side if the latter fires. If all eight rushers come, the weak outside backer would be *free,* and both quarterback and Y must read the strong outside backer's fire, and the ball is dumped immediately to Y. The quarterback must get rid of the football fairly quickly when the rushers outnumber the blockers (Diagram 8-13), should they all come on a tough rush.

Diagram 8-13
Man protection versus split 6 or 4-4 defense.

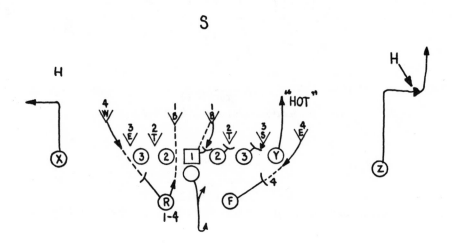

Offensive Passing Strategy Versus the 4-4 Alignment. Relevant to passing strategy versus the Split 6 or 4-4 defense, several observations are worthy of consideration: (1) the use of motion and double wing formations will force the defense to adjust, thus reducing the eight-man rush; (2) sprint-out and action passes, including bootlegs, are better against this alignment than pocket or drop-back passes; (3) if pocket or drop-back passes are utilized, devise patterns where an inside linebacker must cover an offensive back coming out of his backfield; (4) the offense must have receivers who are capable of beating defenders 1-on-1, especially against tough man coverage; (5) the offense must take the calculated risk at times of sending out more than two or three receivers because Split 6 teams do not rush frequently with all eight men, nor do they play 3-deep *man* coverage all the time. The linebackers usually rush in pairs so that six men are coming, instead of eight rushers. Then, too, if a receiver *beats* man coverage, and the quarterback can get the ball to his receiver, it is almost a certain score.

Individual Pass Blocking Techniques

Let us now consider the individual techniques of an offensive lineman in executing *area, zone* and *man* pass blocking assignments when his quarterback is throwing from the pocket.

There are two points-of-view on pass blocking: (1) the hit-and-recoil or *aggressive* technique and (2) the drop-step or *passive* technique. (The term *passive* is somewhat of a misnomer in identifying the technique, but is used merely to denote it is the opposite of the *aggressive* pass blocking technique.)

The Hit-and-Recoil Technique. On the snap of the football, the offensive lineman takes a short jab step with his *back* foot so as to square off with the defender, making contact immediately with an aggressive block which stimulates a double uppercut motion with the fists. Obviously the blocker does *not* strike his opponent with his fists, but such a motion puts the pass protector in the desired position. The contact is more of a pushing motion rather than a striking motion. In the double uppercut motion, the fists come up under the chin, the elbows are in near the protector's waist, his tail is low, his feet should be up under his body, with the hitting motion being up and through. The pass protector must keep his feet moving, free (*clear*) himself immediately from his opponent by backing away from him with quick steps and prepare to "pop" his opponent again. In present-day football, the technique is taught in the following manner: jab step with back foot, square off with opponent, *ping* your man, get away from him and get set to strike again. If the rusher comes tough and strong, the pass protector can use a drop or cut technique by throwing a long body block at the knees-shins of his opponent. If the rusher takes an inside rush, the offensive blocker should shuffle to the inside and stack him up, which will be discussed shortly.

The advantages of the hit-and-recoil technique are that the blocker contacts the rusher immediately on or near the line-of-scrimmage, delays recognition of the pass by the defender and the technique is likely to make the rusher more cautious. Coaches who advocate this method feel the rusher does not have the opportunity to gather momentum in his charge, as may be the case when the pass protector drop steps and shows pass protection immediately. However, the hit-and-recoil technique is probably not used as extensively in present-day football as the drop-step technique.

The Drop-Step Technique. Many coaches feel that since the objective is not to drive the defenders off the line-of-scrimmage, and since the pass is generally thrown from a point *approximately* 6–7 yards behind the line, the offensive linemen need not block out aggressively initially when drop-back passes are being utilized. However, as was pointed out above, those who teach the aggressive method do *not* fire out into the defender and attempt to drive him off the line, but merely square off and strike the rusher at the line-of-scrimmage before retreating quickly. However, probably the main reason aggressive blocking is not being used universally is that by utilizing the drop-step method of pass blocking, the offensive linemen can reduce the effectiveness of line stunts and are less likely to make an error in reading the stunt and blocking their man. Therefore, this technique might be referred to as *passive,* but the blocking becomes aggressive when the rusher declares himself and enters the *combat zone*. If the protection breaks down, the blocker should not lose his poise, but should fight to regain his balance. If he cannot regain his balance, he may *"cut"* the rusher as the last resort.

The method of drop stepping (*"clearing"*) to set up quickly, is as follows: drop step with *inside* foot first, then outside foot, with the latter pointed toward the crotch of the rusher. The blocker should have his elbows in, fists up under his chin, in order to wipe off the rusher's hands if he puts them on the blocker's shoulder pads or headgear. If the elbows are away from the body, the pass rusher will use the elbows as *handles* to turn the blocker and go by him.

The pass protector should keep his feet moving in order to position himself between the defensive rusher and the passer, and to maintain an *inside-out* position on the rusher (working him to the outside). The pass protector cannot be stiff-legged, over-extended nor have his weight back on his heels. His weight should be over his center of gravity, which means he must be well-balanced and have his body in alignment, in a good football position.

Similarities and Differences. In the *aggressive* technique, the blocker engages his rusher right away at the line-of-scrimmage. In the *passive* technique, the blocker drops, makes the rusher show and then engages his man. There is probably very little difference in the techniques initially, and no difference after the first separation, drop-step and set-up. These two techniques apply, however, only to pocket protection where the passer sets up deeper, and does not apply to the quick pass where the passer sets up 1–3 yards in depth.

Quick, Aggressive Protection. The blocker steps into the defender on the snap of the football on quick, aggressive protection, and sustains his block, scrambling to tie up his man. The block is aggressive because the offensive lineman forces the defender to keep his hands down (by playing off the blocker), which does not permit him to deflect the quick pass. Therefore, *quick,* aggressive pass protection is different from the type of aggressive pass protection discussed in the section above. Scramble and reach blocking techniques were discussed previously in Chapter 6, although the latter will be illustrated shortly as a method of pass protection for the sprint-out pass.

Pass Protection Techniques Versus Various Defensive Rushes

Basically, an offensive lineman sets up inside of the pass rusher so as to force him to take an outside rush. When the rusher lines up inside of the offensive blocker, the latter must take a quick shuffle step to the inside to close the inside rush route to the passer. As the blocker sets up, the rusher can take one of three paths—inside, outside or he comes straight.

The Inside Rusher. There are two techniques of blocking the rusher who takes the inside route. Some coaches advocate teaching the offensive blocker to shuffle quickly to his inside, maintaining contact with the defender, jamming him with the *inside* shoulder and knocking him into the next adjacent blocker. The blocker must maintain a good, balanced football position, and shuffle his feet in order to maintain position on the rusher. He cannot lunge at the defender.

Other coaches advocate teaching the blocker, versus the inside rusher, to reverse shoulder block the defender quickly by driving the blocker's head in *front* of the rusher and sustaining contact with the *outside* shoulder. Once again, an effort is made to jam the rusher into an adjacent blocker.

In both techniques, the offensive blocker sustains his block and moves his feet, maintaining leverage on the rusher as long as possible. When he feels he is losing his man, he may throw at the rusher's knees-shins, in an effort to "cut" him. Caution the blocker only to throw as a last resort or the rusher is likely to hurdle the pass protector, especially if the latter goes to the ground.

The Outside Rusher. Should the pass rusher take an outside rush route, by executing his technique properly the blocker can direct the defender out of the play and away from the passer in the pocket.

As the offensive lineman clears and sets quickly, he keeps the pass rusher on the outside. Here, once again, he may execute one of two techniques, depending on what he has been taught.

When the pass rusher cannot cut back to the inside, the blocker pivots and drives his head in *front* of the rusher and reverse shoulder blocks with his *inside* shoulder, driving his man beyond the passer.

The other technique is for the blocker to keep his head on the inside and shoulder block with the *outside* shoulder. In this latter method, the chance for error of the rusher coming back to the inside is less than if the first technique of blocking the outside rusher with the inside shoulder is employed. In the first technique, the blocker must make a judgment decision of when to pivot and run with the outside runner. Should the latter stop, or fake, driving hard like he is coming on an outside rush, and the blocker pivots in order to drive block the outside rush, the offensive lineman could not protect inside should the rusher go behind him.

The Rusher Who Comes Straight. If the rusher comes straight the blocker may use either of the two techniques described previously, depending on how he has been coached. However, he should strive for a slight *inside-out* position on the rusher. Otherwise he stays squared up with the rusher and utilizes either of the techniques as explained above. If the rusher then takes one side or the other on his rush, the offensive blocker follows the procedure just described.

Additional Coaching Points for Pass Protection Techniques

While offensive linemen must be aware of the various areas from where their team's passes will be thrown (pocket, semi-sprint, option run-pass, waggle, bootleg, etc.), and adjust to their position blocks accordingly, a good coaching point is the application of the general rule for offensive linemen: "Point your tail toward your passer and keep your body between him and the rusher!" The successful application of this rule will generally place an offensive lineman in the best position to protect his passer, regardless of where he sets up to pass.

Coping with Fakes. Pass protectors must recognize and know how to cope with fakes. The general rule is to make the pass rusher "show," always respecting the inside fake, but do not commit to the outside fake.

On an outside rush, the blocker must make certain the rusher has reached the point of no return, in that he cannot change direction quickly and come back to the inside on his pass rush. If the offensive blocker goes after the pass rusher too soon on an outside rush, the latter is likely to change direction quickly and come to the inside. If the blocker has committed himself already, in all probability he will be unable to change position quickly enough to prevent the pass rusher from rushing inside.

Engage Rusher, Protect Passer. The offensive linemen should engage the rushers near the line-of-scrimmage, regardless of the technique which is employed. Consequently, a rusher should not be permitted to penetrate more than 1½–2 yards, which means this is the deepest a blocker should retreat in making his stand.

Get the Job Done. The first requisite of pass blocking is the desire to get the job done. A pass protector should never assume his job is complete until the play is blown dead by the referee. Lastly, know whom to block—and then do it!

ACTION OR PLAY PASS PROTECTION BLOCKING TECHNIQUES

Excluding pulling out of the line to protect the passer (Chapter 6), blocking for action or play passes may be broken down into aggressive blocking for the on-side and area blocking for the off-side. Or the pass play, off of the running play fake, may be blocked the same as the running play (with certain modifications).

The Fake Tailback Draw (or Delay) Pass

Diagram 8-14 is the pass off of the fake hand-off to the tailback from the "I" formation, and will be included for the following reasons: (1) the pass is the companion play off the popular tailback draw or delay (Diagram 8-20); (2) both plays are effective versus modern-day defenses; (3) the pass illustrates the techniques indicated above, namely aggressive blocking on the front side and area blocking back side.

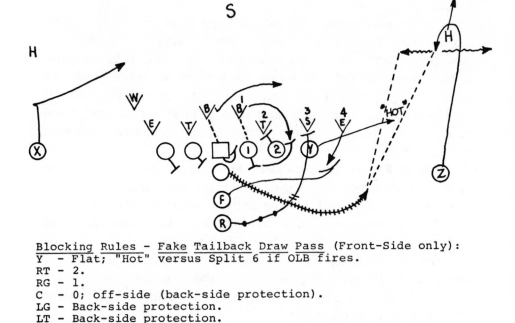

Blocking Rules - Fake Tailback Draw Pass (Front-Side only):
```
Y  - Flat; "Hot" versus Split 6 if OLB fires.
RT - 2.
RG - 1.
C  - 0; off-side (back-side protection).
LG - Back-side protection.
LT - Back-side protection.
X  - Across.
Z  - Hook and slide to get open; go "up" if it's there.
F  - Overblock widest container.
R  - Fake TB Draw, BLOCK widest linebacker (OLB) if he fires.
QB - Fake TB Draw with free hand, lay ball on hip, challenge
     outside. "Y" is "hot" if OLB fires (Split 6 or 4-4 defense).
```

Diagram 8-14

Fake tailback draw pass versus split 6 or 4-4 defense.

The Fake Power Sweep Bootleg and Waggle Passes

To supplement the power sweep (Diagram 6-11), you must have the bootleg pass (Diagram 8-15), which fakes the sweep strong side, and the waggle pass (Diagram 8-16), which fakes the sweep to the weak side. There are several ways of blocking the play, such as actually blocking the power sweep (Diagrams 8-15 to 8-16), or devising special rules to block the defense. Secondly, the sweep (Diagram 6-11), must be thoroughly established both ways or the bootleg and waggle passes will not be effective. Therefore, the faking action of the backfield, with the quarterback going counter to the action and faking the hand-off, should move linebackers and secondary defenders, permitting receivers to get open. Thirdly, the back to whom the quarterback fakes initially, may be assigned as a blocker after faking the sweep action or he may be a safety valve receiver. Lastly, in designing the play, some coaches run the power sweep and the pass off the fake sweep, by employing two tight ends. On the waggle pass, by faking the sweep action away from Z, only X and Z are receivers, and Y remains in as an added blocker. Then X, who is the other tight end, is in a better position to come across on his pattern than he is from a flexed position. On the bootleg action, X, Y and Z are all in the pattern (Diagram 8-15). Both offensive guards will pull to protect the passer if they are uncovered (Diagram 8-16); if covered, only the off-side guard pulls for protection (Diagram 8-15).

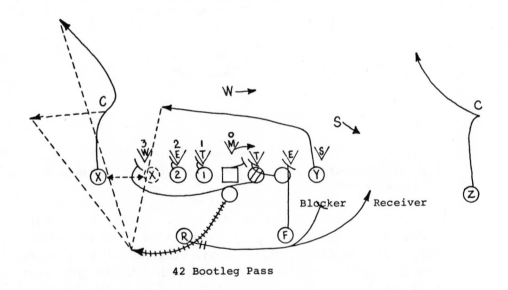

42 Bootleg Pass

Diagram 8-15

Fake power sweep front side versus pro 4-3 defense (42 bootleg pass).

The Keep Pass, Off the Fake Sweep Action

Diagram 8-17 illustrates the keep pass, where the quarterback fakes a hand-off to R, rolls with flow in behind him and generally throws to his fullback in the flat. Diagram 8-17 illustrates the keep pass versus the standard 6-5 goal line defense with *man* coverage in

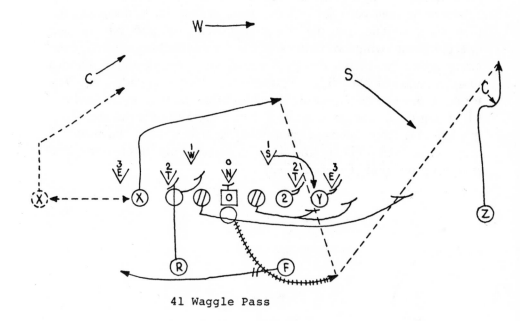

41 Waggle Pass

Diagram 8-16

Fake power sweep weak side versus Oklahoma 5-2 defense (41 waggle pass).

the secondary. This forces the middle linebacker (M) to cover the fullback in the flat, which is extremely difficult for him to do effectively, even from his adjusted position (Diagram 8-17). With the strong-side safety covering Y man-for-man, if the latter releases slowly he can hold S in position and still create a traffic jam for M, making it impossible for the latter to cover him in the flat. Should S switch off to cover F, with M covering Y, the latter should be open immediately.

THE SEMI-SPRINT AND SPRINT-OUT PASSES

In the semi-sprint (Diagram 8-18), the quarterback will set up behind his guard-tackle, and has no intention of challenging the corner for an option run-pass. In Diagrams 4-2 and 4-3, Chapter 4, the passer will challenge the corner (front side and back side, respectively), with a run-pass option.

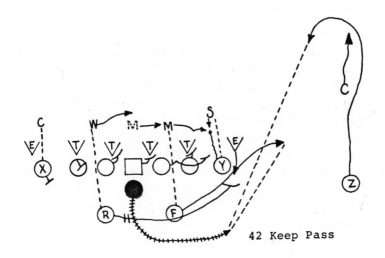

Diagram 8-17

Fake power sweep keep pass front side versus 6-5 goal line defense (42 keep pass).

Diagram 8-18

Semi-sprint-out pass front side (84).

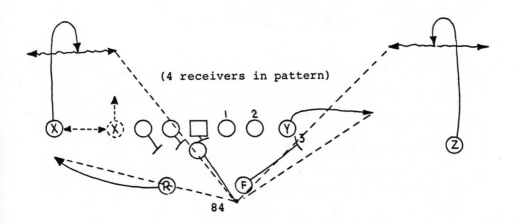

The Semi-Sprint-Out Pass

There are several ways of protecting the passer when he sets up behind his tackle. Diagram 8-18 illustrates the front-side, semi-sprint pass, where the off-side linemen provide back-side protection, and the right guard, tackle and fullback protect front side, with four receivers out. Diagram 8-19 illustrates the left tackle and guard dropping to pick up the back-side rush, with the front-side linemen *reach* blocking for the outside leg of the defenders, with a five-man pass pattern. With one less blocker, but one more receiver (Diagram 8-19), the quarterback must dump the football quickly to his flaring fullback or to Y if the defense comes with a tough rush. The back-side protectors must close to the inside first, before hinging for back-side protection, since the front-side linemen are reach blocking.

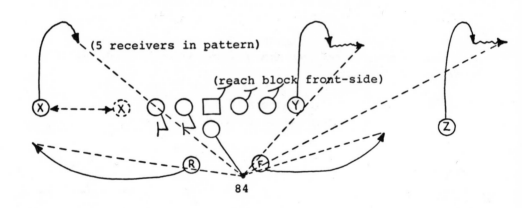

Diagram 8-19
Sprint-out pass front side (84).

The Sprint-Out Option Run-Pass

Diagrams 4-2 and 4-3 (Chapter 4) illustrate the sprint-out run-pass option front and back side, respectively, versus the Split 6 defense.

The Tailback Draw or Delay, and Pass

Since defenders have reduced the effectiveness of the sprint-out option by rapidly reacting in their pursuit to the full flow of the offensive backs, an effective counter-measure, the tailback draw or delay (Diagram 8-20, front side; Diagram 8-21, back side) has been added to present-day football. The ball carrier starts in the direction of backfield flow, but frequently ends up running to daylight by breaking the play to the off-side of the offensive line. The tailback draw or delay is not a typical draw play utilized in the sense that the conventional draw is employed. The tailback draw or delay is an excellent play which may be used on almost any down, especially versus opponents who react quickly and pursue immediately as soon as they read the flow action of the offensive backs.

While there is a pass off of the running fake to the front side (Diagram 8-14), there is not a pass off of the running fake to the back side. It cannot be blocked properly. However, the companion pass is not necessary, and the sequence is effective regardless. The sprint-out pass to the weak side (Diagram 4-3) is utilized instead.

These counter-measures will definitely cut down rapid pursuit and keep defenders at home, or a good running back will gain much yardage running to daylight through areas vacated by quick-reacting linemen and linebackers. The offensive linemen take the defenders in the direction they want to charge or pursue, which frequently leaves voids in the defensive front. Defenders must read the tailback draw or delay properly because they can pursue in the direction of flow. In turn this makes the sprint-out, run-pass option, and the pass off the fake draw first, more effective.

Since Y can split out as he is going to release to the outside on all plays his way, i.e., sprint, draw, pass, and he blocks the safety man on plays away from his side, he can force the defense to adjust fairly easily (end moves in over offensive tackle and linebacker plays outside over offensive end). At times the offensive end will want to force this defensive adjustment, and other times he will not want to force it. Secondly, it is more effective to run the plays to the front or strong side than to run them to the back side of the formation.

Coaching Points for the Tailback Draw or Delay. Linemen will use draw blocking techniques, unless defensive linemen commit immediately. Then the offensive linemen should block the rushers in the direction of their charge. If defensive linemen wait, attempting to read the play and then react to it, offensive blockers should block them aggressively. Where a linebacker moves with flow, he should be blocked in the direction he is moving. In the draw play to the back

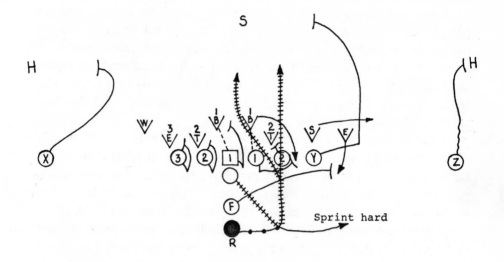

Diagram 8-20
Tailback draw or delay front side versus split 6 or 4-4 defense.

Diagram 8-21
Tailback draw or delay back side versus split 6 or 4-4 defense.

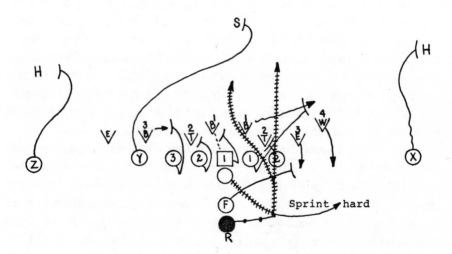

side of the formation (Diagram 8-21) in particular, the *sprint-out* (Diagram 4-3) *must be well established* and be a threat in order to force the defensive contain man to stay at home. He must be "outside conscious" and "contain conscious" or both he and the next defender inside of the *container* (3 and/or 4 men) will pinch to the inside and close off the tailback draw or delay.

THE DRAW PLAY

In order to keep the defense honest, and to make the passing attack more effective, a coach must incorporate the draw play and the screen pass as part of his offensive attack. Both the draw and screen should be devised in such a manner as to tie in with the overall passing scheme. As an illustration, if straight drop-back passing is an integral part of the offensive attack, then the draw and screen should also be run off of straight drop-back action. Conversely, if straight drop-back passing is *not* an integral part of the attack, but semi-sprint-out passing is, then the draw and screen should be run off of the latter action. To run the draw and screen off of drop-back action, when it is not an integral part of a coach's offensive attack, would be very questionable and not likely be too effective.

The same principle applies as to the type of line blocking which will be utilized for the draw play in particular. As an illustration, if turn-out blocking is being employed in the line when the quarterback throws from the pocket (Diagrams 8-6 to 8-7), then turn-out blocking should be used for the draw play.

The most conventional type of play has draw blocking in the line and split blocking in the backfield, with the quarterback slipping the football to one of his backs. Diagram 8-22 illustrates the draw to the fullback off of semi-sprint (or drop-back) action in the backfield and draw blocking in the line. This ties in with the screen pass to R (Diagram 8-23) off of the same action versus the 4-3 defensive alignment.

Diagram 8-22 illustrates the interior linemen responsible for the middle five defenders, with the center and weak-side guard *switch* blocking versus an even alignment (center blocks 0 in odd) and Y releasing through 3 to block safety. The wide flankers release, run pattern and block the most dangerous defender. R blocks 3 his side. The fullback should wait, read the line blocking and then run to daylight!

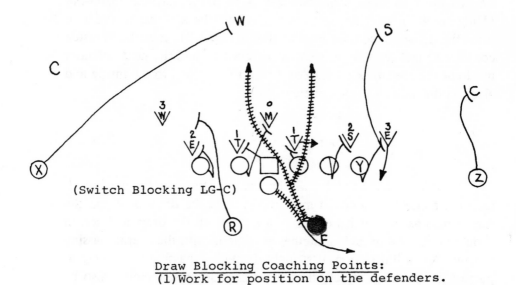

(Switch Blocking LG-C)

Draw Blocking Coaching Points:
(1) Work for position on the defenders.
(2) Take defenders in direction of their charge.
(3) Keep middle open - work from inside-out.

Diagram 8-22
Draw right to fullback versus 4-3, eagle adjustment.

THE SCREEN PASS

The screen pass may be thrown off of drop-back, sprint-out or play action by the quarterback. Diagram 8-23 illustrates the screen pass to R off of semi-sprint action, although it could just as well be thrown off of straight drop-back action. Diagram 8-24 illustrates a different type of screen, in that it is thrown to the *second* man coming out of the backfield, which makes it very effective and is difficult for the defenders to cover, especially if they are in man coverage in the secondary (with the strong linebacker on the fullback). The latter is a "slip screen" to the fullback and may be thrown off of either semi-sprint or straight drop-back action by the quarterback.

In Diagram 8-23, X, Y and Z all release and block the most dangerous defenders downfield. The off-side (right) guard and tackle block their respective men, with the left tackle, guard and offensive center forming the screen for their receiver, after having bumped their respective men for three counts—1000/1, 1000/2, 1000/3—and then blocking in the screen as indicated. Each lineman should utilize

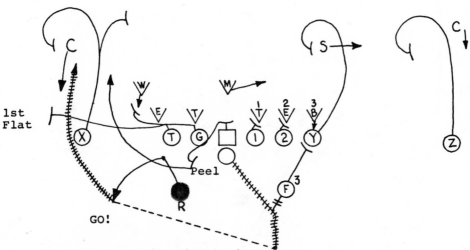

1st
Flat

GO!

Blocking Rules for Linemen in Screen:
T - pull and block most dangerous defender in flat.
G - pull and lead through, blocking 1st defender to show inside.
C - pull and peel back on any rusher threatening R, otherwise
    lead the ball carrier downfield and block. (Some coaches
    reverse blocking assignments for guard and tackle.)

Diagram 8-23
Fake draw right, screen left to R versus pro 4-3 defense.

a shoulder block in carrying out his assignment; the techniques have
been discussed previously.

In Diagram 8-24, only one blocker (left guard) releases in front
of the receiver (fullback). The left tackle drop steps, then cuts down
the defensive end. R blocks the weak-side linebacker, and the fullback
should bump the left guard's man and slip either inside or outside of
the defensive end.

COVERING PASSES

The importance of linemen covering passes was discussed in
Chapter 4.

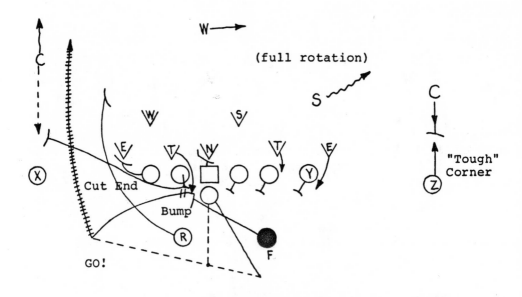

Diagram 8-24

(*Slip*) *screen left* (*weak side*) *to second man* (*FB*) *out of backfield versus Oklahoma 5-2 defense.*

SELECTED DRILLS REFERENCE*

(*See* footnote source for football drills for teaching pass blocking fundamentals, skills and techniques.)

* Donald E. Fuoss, *Championship Football Drills for Teaching Offensive and Defensive Fundamentals and Techniques* (Englewood Cliffs, N.J.: Prentice-Hall, Inc., 1964), pp. 73-74, 80-84.

III

COACHING DEFENSIVE LINEMEN/LINEBACKERS

INTRODUCTION

The basic defensive line play principles and fundamentals which must be taught will be considered first, followed by a discussion of the techniques defensive linemen should employ. Pass rush techniques will be discussed separately (Chapter 11), as will be tackling techniques (Chapter 13). End play techniques which are different from those of the other defensive linemen will be presented in Chapter 10, and linebacker techniques in Chapter 12.

PROPER ALIGNMENT

Proper alignment is very important, and should be as accurate as possible so that a defensive player can carry out his assignment and responsibilities. An individual's defensive alignment depends upon the theory of the particular defense which is being employed and his specific defensive responsibilities; i.e., off-set, gap, nose-on, control an opponent, control one side of an opponent, etc.

If a defensive player does not know where to line up properly or he is careless or indifferent about his correct alignment, there is little need to go further with other fundamentals, because he is already at a disadvantage due to his erroneous alignment. For this reason, *proper* alignment heads the list of defensive fundamentals, although individual stance is taught first.

Coaching Defensive Line Fundamentals, Skills and Techniques

STANCE FOR DEFENSIVE LINEMEN

Defensive line play begins with a good stance, although there is a difference of opinion among coaches as to whether a three-point or four-point stance is the best for internal linemen.

Advantages, Disadvantages of Three- and Four-Point Stances

A four-point stance enables a lineman to play lower, gives better balance and permits a better and stronger forward charge. A three-point stance might be more adaptable for a lineman to strike a blow, especially if he is looping and slanting in his defensive charge. Therefore, an interior lineman may employ either a three- or four-point defensive stance, depending upon his preference, physical capabilities and particular duties and responsibilities. Since there are different body types, not every player can be molded into one exact stance. Therefore, individual differences and physical capabilities must be recognized and taken into consideration. A player should be permitted to take the most natural and comfortable stance possible, as long as he can carry out his duties and responsibilities.

A Suggested Stance

A good fundamental stance for defensive internal linemen has the following elements:

1. Optional three- or four-point stance (similar to the one that is taught offensively).
2. Feet approximately shoulder width apart, staggered not more than toe-to-heel.
3. Weight distributed on the balls of the feet, with slightly more weight forward on the down hand(s) than on the feet.
4. Down hand(s) 4–6" out in front of the head (off-hand hanging, with elbow slightly bent in front of knee).
5. Knees flexed, with the tail approximately over the ankles or heels.
6. Hips and shoulders at the *approximate* same level (individual matter), but both parallel with the line-of-scrimmage.
7. Back parallel (or almost parallel, depending on elevation of shoulders and/or hips) with the ground, head up, eyes forward.

From this basic stance there will be individual deviations by both player and coach, for the reasons cited previously. Regardless of these, from his defensive stance a lineman must be taught to lead step with either foot first, and as he strikes a blow his feet must be brought up under him.

The amount of weight forward on the down hand, as an illustration, depends on whether the defensive lineman is always charging straight ahead or varying his defensive charge, looping, slanting, veering, etc. While he should not noticeably vary the amount of weight on his down hand(s), tipping off the type of charge he is going to employ (with the exception of when he is taking a gap or goal line charge and wants penetration), if he has too much weight forward he will encounter difficulty when he is stunting. Regardless of an individual's stance, he must be able to move quickly on the initial movement of the blocker opposite him or on the movement of the football, or he will be outcharged.

MOVEMENT

There is also a difference of opinion among coaches as to whether the defensive lineman should move on the initial movement of the player opposite him or on the movement of the football. Some players are in closer proximity to the football and can view both their opponent and the ball. They can move on their opponent's movement and/or the movement of the ball.

If a defensive lineman cannot see both the ball and his opponent through split vision, then he should watch his opponent and move on his movement, especially if playing a straight-ahead, hit-and-hunt type of defensive play. If defensive line stunts are being employed and the linemen are slanting, looping and veering, then they might have to watch the football, although this is a contrary point-of-view held by some coaches. However, if a defensive lineman will watch the down hand of his opponent closely and move when his opponent raises his hand to charge, the defender will be able to step and hit or strike a blow immediately. Consequently, the offensive blocker will not outcharge the defensive lineman.

When the opposition's down hand moves, the defender should literally *sprint* or *explode* into the blocker, depending on the technique being employed, which will depend on such factors as the tactical situation and the philosophy of the defensive coach (lift versus shiver). In any case, the defender should get to the blocker first and deliver his blow rather than *catching* the blocker's. Football is a game of contact, and it is either hit or be hit, especially in line play.

HIT OR BLOCK PROTECTION

It is a well-known fact that football games are won and lost in the line, and the player who establishes physical toughness or supremacy immediately, will generally control that particular piece of territory. Thus, it is essential that hitting or striking a blow be one of the basic fundamentals of defensive line play.

Elements of "Hitting" Techniques

The hand shiver and forearm lift techniques, the two basic hitting techniques for defensive linemen, will be explained shortly. However, the general elements in both hitting techniques are as follows:

1. All movement with the hands and arms is forward, and the blow is delivered with quickness.
2. Defeat the offensive blocker on the line-of-scrimmage, neutralize his charge and control assigned territory.
3. End up in a balanced position, with the feet up under the body and moving, parallel and even with each other, and shoulders parallel with the line-of-scrimmage.

The inexperienced player in particular is likely to forget the necessity of first stepping and delivering a blow into his opponent, in order to carry out the other fundamentals of defensive line play.

PROTECT AREA AND FIGHT PRESSURE

The defender must neutralize the offensive charge of the blocker so that he will control his assigned territory. The offensive team cannot make yardage through any area of the line if every defensive lineman plays his position properly and is not whipped by his offensive blocker. Each player should be made to feel that his particular territory or area of responsibility is the most important area in his team's coordinated defense, and it is necessary for each player to protect his territory. All players know they will be blocked at times, but the good player does not stay blocked. Every player should play his position first, fight pressure and then react.

Each defender must locate the football or the ball carrier as quickly as possible. If a defender will fight pressure and play through resistance, instead of looking into the backfield and watching the action there, he will not be fooled by the backfield action faking techniques. A defensive lineman must move first, deliver a blow and then locate the football before reacting.

LOCATE FOOTBALL AND REACT PROPERLY

The *proper reaction* for a defensive player may be relatively simple to explain, but it takes much time, drill and practice to get the proper coordination of eye, mind and body for the correct response. The defender's reactions after his defensive charge depend on whether the football is coming toward him or going away from his defensive position. A defensive lineman must be taught to *read the blocking scheme* in order to react properly, which is illustrated and will be discussed shortly.

A common error for the inexperienced player is to attempt to locate the football without first delivering a blow. He must neutralize the blocker, and he cannot do this without first delivering a blow to his opponent to keep the blocker from getting into his block protection area. Or he will "take" the backfield fake and leave his area unprotected. The defensive lineman's key is in the immediate area of the blocker opposite him and those linemen to either side. This is why he must be taught to read the blocking scheme or "the triangle," in order to react properly. Although a defensive lineman may be fooled at times by influence blocking (Diagram 6-15), if he will react to his key and locate the ball carrier or the football, his defensive play will be sound. If he ignores his key and watches the play of the offensive backs, he probably will be fooled many times.

SHED AND RELEASE

A defensive lineman's job is to control his man, protect his assigned territory, find the football, get to it and make the tackle. Therefore, a defender must shed and release from his blocker as quickly as possible.

The inexperienced and/or undisciplined defensive player may become so engrossed in beating his opponent physically that he wins the individual battle but loses the *war*. Frequently such a defender is still trying to whip his blocker at the line-of-scrimmage, despite the fact the opposing ball carrier is well beyond his area of play. When this occurs, for all practical purposes the blocker has executed the perfect block, since the defensive lineman is totally removed from the play and is not in the pursuit pattern at all.

Use Both Hands to Shed and Release

Secondly, the defender must be taught to use both hands to shed the blocker and release from him. If the defensive lineman is using a lift or the flipper, the inexperienced and undisciplined player, although having a good hit or blow, has a tendency to remain close to his opponent. A poor blocker inevitably will grab a defender's arm and hold him or get to his legs and tie him up, because his opponent is close in to him.

The defender should bring up his off-hand to shed and ward off the blocker and disengage from him, getting *operating space* between himself and the blocker, regardless of the hitting technique he employs. "Quick" feet come into play here, because the defender must square off and keep the blocker away from his legs.

In order to shed and release, the interior lineman should hit and slide laterally, shoulders square with the line-of-scrimmage, in order to keep the ball carrier from breaking back to the inside through an opening. Then, too, the defenders want to meet the ball carrier in the hole square, and not at an angle, in the event the ball carrier runs to daylight to the inside.

CONTAIN THE BALL CARRIER

While defensive ends or others in the defensive perimeter are generally responsible for containment, which will be discussed in Chapter 10, on occasion tackles and linebackers are charged with it. Pursuit cannot be discussed properly without first stressing the importance of containing the ball carrier. Pursuit is practically worthless if containment is lost. You must work on containing the ball carrier at all times. If you do not contain properly, you cannot play winning defensive football.

PROPER PURSUIT

Proper pursuit is probably the most important fundamental in defensive football today; every defender must know and understand both the importance of this fundamental and the correct angle of pursuit. Pursuit should be relentless by all 11 men. Players must be coached in the proper angle of pursuit because this fundamental of defensive play is probably violated more than any other. Pursuit is the winning edge in football, and it is nothing more than each player getting to the spot where he is going to make the tackle as quickly as possible. The backbone of great defensive football teams is outstanding pursuit.

Basic Elements of Pursuit

The basic elements of proper pursuit involve judgment and each defender's own abilities. Quickness and running ability are the most important factors, and for defensive linemen and linebackers they must be able to pick up their feet, not like in a track meet, but in moving over and around obstacles. (This does not mean running around a blocker.) The speed with which defensive linemen and linebackers get into the correct pursuit pattern depends on how quickly each defender can "read the blocking scheme" or read through the blocker to the football.

As was mentioned previously, defensive linemen should keep their hips and shoulders parallel with the line-of-scrimmage when moving laterally, for the reasons mentioned previously, in order to take away the cut-back by the ball carrier.

In addition to judgment and individual abilities of each player, the correct angle of pursuit depends on a number of variable factors— such as whether the play is to the long side or short side of the field; toward or away from the individual defender or the point-of-attack and the defender's proximity to it; each individual defender's speed versus the ball carrier's ability and speed; etc.

Proper Pursuit Must Be Coached

Players must be coached in the *proper* angle of pursuit. Coaching the correct angle on every defensive play in practice is the only way to get satisfactory execution during a game. It must be fused into the overall defense or a coach will never be able to defend against all of the different offensive sets and plays his team is likely to encounter. Briefly, the further the defensive man is from the critical point-of-attack where the ball crosses the line-of-scrimmage, the greater is his angle of departure from the line-of-scrimmage. Each defender as he pursues should be a yard deeper than the man pursuing in front of him, so that one block cannot eliminate two defenders (i.e., don't get tied up in a *traffic jam* of bodies). As the man in front closes to the ball the next pursuer should close too, so as not to create a cut-back lane for the ball carrier. As each individual defender pursues, he should look at the ball carrier and adjust on him. All pursuers should be spread out in an *organized* pattern, and not be trailing one another.

Never Stay Blocked—Take Proper Pursuit Angle

A defensive man may be blocked, but a good one never stays blocked. He should recover as quickly as possible, react properly and begin his proper pursuit pattern. If a defensive player starts his pursuit at the wrong angle, he immediately eliminates himself, as he is running an inside arc and chasing the ball carrier from behind with no chance of heading him off. One defender on the side removed or away from the flow of the play generally is designated as a *"chase"* man to take care of the reverse, the bootleg to the off-side, the broken play or cut-back behind the line-of-scrimmage, etc. (Chapter 10).

Pursue, Don't Chase

Such errors as penetrating too deeply, running around blocks and taking an inside arc places the defender in the position of a *chaser* instead of a pursuer, with no chance of heading off the ball carrier downfield. This is individual defensive play and is not coordinated team play, which contributes toward the long run for the opposition.

Defenders must go to the football with agility, and use the side-line to trap the ball carrier.

MAKE THE TACKLE!

Making the tackle is, the final and most satisfying phase of defensive football; everything else is in vain if the defender gets that far, then misses the tackle. Tackling fundamentals and techniques will be discussed in Chapter 13.

Now let us analyze the defensive techniques which linemen will utilize in applying the principles and fundamentals of defensive line play.

HAND SHIVER TECHNIQUES

The basic technique of defensive line play is the use of the hands for protection. These are a defensive player's tools, and he must learn how to use them properly in order to keep blockers away from his body.

The hand shiver consists of stepping with the rear foot and hitting with the palms and heels of the hands simultaneously, under the shoulders or to the chest or head of the opponent, depending on the elevation of the blocker as he comes off the line-of-scrimmage, in order to straighten him up, breaking and neutralizing his charge. The blow must be delivered through the blocker and beyond in order to get *operating space* between the defender and the blocker.

Wrists and Elbows Should Be Locked

The feet should be parallel and even when the hands and arms are extended forward. The wrists and elbows must be locked in order to deliver the blow with strength and authority. Otherwise the offensive player's charge will collapse the arms of the defender, who can then get at the latter's legs with a shoulder block. As the hands strike forward, the defender should dip his tail and snap his head back to insure balance, with his feet under his body.

The blow must be delivered from under the blocker, and the defensive lineman must follow through with short, driving steps until the ball is located or until he determines from where pressure is being exerted.

The Shiver Is a Good Hit-and-Hunt Technique. Unless a defender is physically superior to his opponent, it is difficult to get much penetration with a shiver charge. However, a defensive lineman can pursue faster when using the hand shiver as compared to the forearm lift or the shoulder charge. Although it is difficult to punish the blocker physically with a hand shiver, it does permit the defender to get *operating space* and keep the blocker away from his legs. This does not imply the defender should not *hit,* because he should deliver a blow to the blocker with a shiver or a lift and literally try to knock off his tail if at all possible without losing sight of his objective, which is to get to the ball carrier as quickly as possible and make the tackle.

A slight variation of the above-described shiver technique, referred to as a *tough* shiver technique, will be discussed shortly. This does not imply the conventional technique is a *soft* shiver, because such a method would not be effective and is not taught.

FOREARM LIFT TECHNIQUES

When employing the lift or flipper, the shoulder and forearm should be coordinated with the same foot in order to give the strongest possible position. In the conventional technique, the defensive lineman takes a short step forward with either foot and uncoils with the same shoulder and forearm, delivering a blow to his opponent. The blow is actually struck with the back of the hand and forearm to the pit of the stomach or chest of the blocker, depending once again on the elevation of the offensive player as he comes off of the line-of-scrimmage on his offensive charge. The opposite hand is used for leverage on the blocker, destroying his body balance and keeping him away from the defender.

Work the Feet

It is important that the forearm be delivered up through the blocker. The defender should not hit too high or he will go over the blocker and is likely to be blocked. After delivering the forearm lift, the defender should come off of the blocker, working his feet in short, choppy steps, and be ready to react to pressure and the football.

If a defender is nose-up on his opponent, as would be the case of a nose defender in an odd alignment or defenders on the guards in a 4-3 alignment, and he employs a forearm or shoulder lift, he must square up quickly, maintain leverage and keep the blocker away from his legs and body. Generally, the defender favors one side or the other when he employs a lift technique from a nose-up position. If the blocker gets into the defender at all, he can seal off his man and practically eliminate the defender from the pursuit pattern. Therefore, as the defender slams the blocker with his lift technique, he should drop his hips, snap back his head, have his feet up under his body, work his feet and be ready to react to pressure or to the football, just as he does when employing the hand shiver. As illustrated in Diagram 9-1, the defender must be able to key the offensive blockers to each side of the opponent opposite him (whether he is nose-up or off-set), and be prepared to "read the blocking scheme" or "read the triangle."

SHOULDER CHARGE TECHNIQUES

A shoulder charge technique is generally used in a short yardage situation, especially when the defense wants to meet force with force, as when near the goal line. Pursuit is limited, as the defender literally buries himself since he and the blocker use the same technique, in that each tries to shoulder block the other. The defender's specific defensive assignment might be to take an outside shoulder, and both

Read/React to Blockers in Your Immediate Area

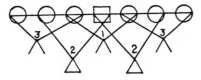

Oklahoma 5-2 Defense

Pro 4-3 Defense

Diagram 9-1
Reading the triangle/blocking scheme.

defender and blocker end up headgear-to-headgear trying to block each other. Or the defender's assignment might be to shoulder charge the inside or outside knee or thigh of his opponent, with his assignment being to gain penetration and make a pile in order to force the ball carrier to belly back should the point-of-attack be toward the specific defender. If the play is away from the defender's position pursuit will be difficult, but the defender should attempt to pursue after carrying out his shoulder charge assignment.

The shoulder charge techniques will be the same as those described for the lift techniques—near foot/near shoulder or step with "off" foot first and then near foot/near shoulder coordinated for the shoulder block, depending on what is taught.

"Tough" Shiver Charge Technique

Mention was made previously of a *tough* shiver technique, which is a surprising change-of-pace for the nose-man to employ when opposite the offensive center. The defender rams into the center hard, *but-*

ting him with his headgear, shiver techniques with his hands on the pads of his opponent and tries to knock the center back into the quarterback and/or force a fumble. The defender goes headgear-to-headgear with the center, but does *not* try to submarine under his opponent. If the nose-man gets too low, the center, although generally surprised by this change-up tactic, might recover his balance and simply fall on the defender and bury him. The only time the nose-man should attempt to go under the offensive center is when he reads wedge block and has no other recourse when confronted with this situation, which will be discussed shortly.

As pointed out in Chapter 5, if the defender over the offensive center can drive the latter into the quarterback, regardless of the defensive technique which he employs, the defender need not vary his tactics because he will literally stop the offense single-handed.

SLANT CHARGE TECHNIQUES

When a defensive lineman varies his charge by stunting, he creates a different problem for the offense. The cross or slant charge is one method of accomplishing this objective, and another is a loop charge technique, both of which are illustrated in Diagram 9-2.

When an interior lineman slant charges, he generally goes from a head-up position on one man to the next opponent adjacent to his position. He might have to move back off the ball to get to his area of responsibility with either a lead or cross-over step. His "cheat" should not be too obvious so that he tips off his intended charge. He must get to his area of responsibility, which depends on the theory of the stunt, in order for the pattern defense or stunt to be sound. He then must react to pressure and the football. A cross-over step will permit the defender to cover more distance in getting to his area of responsibility on his slant charge, but a lead step is more conventional and is more widely taught. The remainder of the technique is merely a shoulder charge into the opponent in the direction the defender is slanting.

Diagram 9-2 illustrates the defensive left tackle taking a slant charge, with the nose-man and right tackle taking a half and full loop charge, respectively. The left illustration shows the offensive play going in the same direction as the defensive charge, and the right illustration shows the play going away from the direction the defensive linemen are charging. In the former, the defensive linemen accelerate their charge to "pursue to the ball carrier," and in the latter, after charging to their point of responsibility, they decelerate as quickly as possible after their initial movement in order to take the *proper* pursuit angle to the football. If slanting or looping, the defender should be permitted to take the quickest and possibly the shortest path to the football, and he may utilize the "quick around" technique if he has looped away initially (Diagram 9-2).

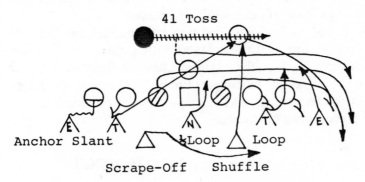

Stunt in Direction of Play

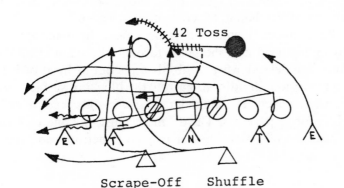

Stunt Away from Direction of Play

Diagram 9-2
Charge to point of responsibility, react, take proper pursuit angle.

LOOP CHARGE TECHNIQUES

The loop charge is another tactic or method of destroying or disrupting an offensive blocking pattern. Probably the most conventional technique of looping is for the defender to step laterally, not turning his body, from his nose-up position to the next man (full loop) or to the gap (half loop), as illustrated in Diagram 9-2. He must move quickly to avoid being blocked by the opponent directly opposite him, and he must deliver a blow with force and authority into the next opponent if he is taking a full loop, to keep from being driven back and literally blown off the line-of-scrimmage.

A second method is to lead step with the foot parallel to the line-of-scrimmage, just as if the defender were pulling out on offense, and then deliver a blow to the adjacent offensive lineman with the head-gear and shoulder lift technique. From this position the defender adheres to the techniques and principles explained previously, and reacts to pressure and the football.

SEAM OR GAP CHARGE TECHNIQUES

The defender either lines up in the seam or from head-up goes to the gap or seam on his initial charge, attempting to get 1½ yards penetration. In this specific situation usually a four-point stance is employed, hips elevated higher than shoulders, with more weight forward on the hands than in the conventional stance.

On the offensive lineman's first movement the defender fires forward, driving his head and shoulders through the seam at hip level of the blocker. The defender fires with his arms out in front of his body, looking to the inside, in order to narrow the blocking surface available to the offensive player. The defender must bring his feet under him as he scrambles for penetration. The defender must rely on quickness and hustle to beat the offensive blocker to gain penetration on the initial charge.

READING/REACTING TO THE BLOCKING SCHEME

For every offensive action there is a proper prescribed reaction by the defender. After having delivered the blow to the offensive blocker, the defender must protect his area and then react in a prescribed manner.

Reaction Versus Single Blocker's Initial Move

First, a defender must be able to react against a single blocker's initial move. As has been pointed out previously, at times a defender will be blocked, but a good defender never stays blocked! When the blocker gets into the defender, the latter must fight through pressure, the blocker's head, in order to try to control him (Diagram 9-3). The defender should not permit himself to be turned to either side, although he might have to give up ground grudgingly, retreating straight back. At times there will be physical mis-matches between blocker and defender, but even though the latter might be driven off the line-of-scrimmage, as long as he is not turned to either side, he still has a chance to jam up the ball carrier. Should he be turned to either side, the defender leaves a void in the defensive alignment and eliminates himself from the pursuit pattern if the point-of-attack is away from his position.

Diagram 9-3

Hit-and-hunt technique, react to pressure.

Take the Most Direct Pursuit Route to the Football. When employing the hit-and-hunt technique, the shiver, lift and even the shoulder charge, the defender must be disciplined not to run around his blocker. While the defender will guess correctly on occasion when the ball carrier breaks his way as he runs around the blocker, more often than not the defender becomes a *chaser* instead of a *pursuer*. Here, once again, he leaves a void in the defense, opens up a running lane for the ball carrier and does not have an opportunity to head off the ball carrier downfield.

While a defender cannot do his job on the ground, he must play with reckless abandon. He must learn to control his own body and throw himself into a hole to make the tackle, and also to go over another defender to get to the ball carrier in order to plug up and jam up inside running plays. He must be taught to neutralize the blocker, control him, break laterally in the direction of the ball carrier as the latter attempts to break off his blocker and make the tackle. If the defender is more powerful than the blocker, then he merely over-powers his man and goes through the blocker to tackle the ball carrier. He must use whatever means possible to get to the ball carrier and make the tackle!

SPLIT 'EM TECHNIQUES

In defensive line play, seldom does an interior lineman play against a single blocker. At times he will be double-teamed, and on a wedge play, a single defender might have to try to fight off three blockers. When a defender is double-teamed, he still must strike a blow, control his man, protect his territory and then react to pressure and find the football. Basically, the defender in such a situation has two techniques; namely, split 'em or pivot out. The elements of both techniques are to deliver a blow to the post blocker, react and *never* try to play both blockers at the same time.

The better of the two techniques, if the defender is a quick-reacting player and has the necessary size and strength, is to split the double-team. If the defender is not quick and/or has been double-teamed, pivoting out (Diagram 9-5) is just about the only way he can get into his pursuit of the ball carrier. In either technique, he is probably not going to get a great deal of pursuit. However, his defensive play will be effective if he makes a pile, gains some penetration and is not moved laterally down the line.

In both techniques, the defender must play the post man first. When the defender feels pressure coming from the lead man, he should immediately direct his attention to him and not attempt to fight both blockers. There are several methods he may use to split 'em.

Forearm Lift Technique

Diagram 9-4 (left illustration) is one such technique, where the defender delivers a forearm lift into the lead blocker a fraction of a second after initially having delivered a blow into the post blocker. The defender employs a forearm lift, stepping with the near (left) leg and slamming with the near (left) forearm, squaring up with the lead blocker, as was described previously.

Diagram 9-4
Techniques for splitting lead-post block.

 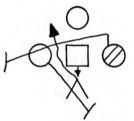

Flipper – Driver   Submarine

Submarine Technique

A second technique of splitting the double-team block is for the defender, upon reading the double-team, to submarine his body quickly into the seam between the two blockers. He should *not* lie on the ground on his stomach in an extended position, but must uncoil, spring to his feet quickly and come back up into the pursuit pattern (Diagram 9-4, right illustration). Frequently his quick-dipping movement will put him under the blockers, who go over the back of the defender. However, if he lies there and does not scramble forward, the blockers will bury the defender by falling on him.

The submarine technique is a good change-up for "splitting 'em," especially if the defender is using both techniques of reacting to the double-team and the pivot-out technique, which will be discussed shortly.

The defender, such as the nose-man in an odd alignment, has very little recourse if a wedge play is directed at him, except to submarine. The best he can do is make a pile. If he is lower than the offensive players, it is likely they will go over his back or fall on the defender. If he is too high they will drive him off the line, and if he mis-reads the wedge as a double-team block and rolls or pivots out (Diagram 9-5), he will open a big running lane for the ball carrier. If he submarines, as described previously, he might split the blockers and possibly make the tackle. Or he will at least pile up the play if he is lower than the wedge blockers.

ROLL OR PIVOT-OUT TECHNIQUES

Another technique for releasing from a double-team block is to spin, roll or pivot out, which is a good method for the defender to utilize if he is slow in his reaction to split 'em, or when he does not have the strength or size to split 'em.

The defender explodes into the post blocker with a shiver or lift, and then reads the double-team block by the lead or drive blocker. Basically, the defender merely reverses, spins or pivots out when he feels pressure, stays low, keeps his feet and goes to the football. One method or the other should be taught for pivoting out. There would not be any need or logic for a coach to teach both of the following methods.

The simplest method is for the defender to drop the foot (left foot in Diagram 9-5) nearest the lead blocker, drive his far (right) elbow behind his back and execute a complete spin through the lead blocker's head.

Or some coaches teach the defender to collapse the knee inward (left knee in Diagram 9-5), which is receiving the pressure, drop step with the away (right) foot from pressure and drive the far (right) elbow behind the back to assist in the quick roll around the blocker's head. He should maintain a low center of gravity and use the offensive blocker for leverage if possible as the defender finishes the execution of his pivot or spin-out technique, squared up in a good football position.

Diagram 9-5
Pivot-out technique versus lead-post block (40 trap).

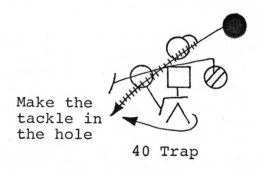

Make the
tackle in
the hole

40 Trap

SELECTED DRILLS REFERENCE

[*See* footnote source for 35 drills for teaching defensive line fundamentals, skills and techniques.* (For a discussion by the author of defensive philosophy; reasons for stemming and stunting; factors governing use of multiple alignments, stunts, coverages; objectives of defensive football; stunts, techniques, variations; pattern stunts; etc.— *see* second footnote source.)]**

---

* Donald E. Fuoss, *Championship Football Drills for Teaching Offensive and Defensive Fundamentals and Techniques* (Englewood Cliffs, N.J.: Prentice-Hall, Inc., 1964), pp. 220-236.

** Donald E. Fuoss, "Purdue's Coordinated Defensive Line Play Techniques and Stunts," *Summer Manual,* American Football Coaches Association, June 1967, pp. 33-40.

INTRODUCTION

With the exception of the defensive secondary, a team can probably get into more trouble with poor defensive end play than any other position. Such reasoning is not illogical.

First, being on the end of the defensive line, the end has the most territory to protect. Basically, in present-day football, the defensive end is usually charged with containment, keeping the play inside and aggressively rushing the passer. An end must be capable of taking on as many blockers as the opposition sends at him in their effort to try to control the corner. Therefore, an individual breakdown in defensive end play opens the door for the long gainer and/or the easy touchdown through the end's unprotected territory.

Multiple Learning-Execution Techniques and Responsibilities

Secondly, the multiple duties and responsibilities of modern-day defenses in stopping high-scoring offenses puts more pressure on the end than on any other defensive lineman. As an illustration, the present-day popular option plays (true Split-T option, belly, Wishbone, triple and/or counter-option) all must be defensed with definite responsibilities fixed from every alignment and stunt. The individual duties and responsibilities are *not* the same all of the time in defensing the option plays. Not only

10

Coaching Defensive End Play Fundamentals, Skills and Techniques

190

does this create multiple teaching-coaching problems for the coach, but also it presents multiple learning-execution problems for the defensive end. The defense (and stunt) dictates alignment, responsibilities and reactions. In modern-day football they change frequently, for the defensive end in particular.

Defensive End Personnel

Thirdly, a defensive end must be a good athlete because of the demands placed on him. Outstanding performances by the players in this position will be important to the success of any defensive team. The defensive end should have the strength and toughness of an interior lineman, but he also needs the agility and quickness of a linebacker. In the selection of your defensive line personnel, the defensive ends should probably receive first consideration after the selection of your linebackers.

The defensive end must adhere to all of the principles, fundamentals and techniques of the other defensive linemen (Chapter 9). Therefore, only differences in defensive end play will be included in this chapter.

A Changing Emphasis

The present-day emphasis on the passing game has forced a change in defensive thinking, which in turn has forced a change in defensive end techniques in particular. While many teams may still employ the Oklahoma 5-2 defense, probably few teams still align and play as *basic,* the static, hanging type of defensive end play which was so prevalent previously. (*See* footnote source for a discussion on "Defensive End Play.")* This is especially true in passing situations or versus passing teams. Defensive thinking presently is to employ three or four linebackers (i.e., the 4-3 or 4-4 alignment) and rush the ends immediately in an aggressive force-contain. In these popular defenses, the linebackers are aligned initially to give more immediate and better underneath pass coverage, and present-day football demands this, too.

From a wider alignment than in the *original* Oklahoma 5-2, where the defensive ends played an outside shade on the offensive ends and helped close the off-tackle hole, present-day defensive ends can aggressively force-contain the play better, and can put greater pressure

---

* Donald E. Fuoss, "Defensive End Play," *Proceeding,* American Football Coaches Association, January 1960, pp. 58-65.

on the passer more quickly. Therefore, almost regardless of the defense, the ends are aligned wider than previously.

DEFENSIVE END STANCE AND ALIGNMENT

The stance of your defensive end will depend upon his assignment and responsibilities. If he is playing basically a wide or loose technique, then he can probably operate best from a two-point upright stance where he can look into the offensive backfield and watch his key. If he has pass coverage responsibilities and/or he is stunting, he can do this better from an upright stance, too. Therefore, on occasion the end will employ an upright stance.

When the defensive end's responsibility is to penetrate to a point on a controlled charge—force-contain, keep the offensive play inside or force it deep and/or pressure the passer—he can do this best from a down or three-point stance. Therefore, he will be utilizing a three-point stance, too.

Irregardless, the end's cardinal rule is, "Never be hooked." Therefore, his alignment will depend not only on the defense (stunt) and his responsibilities, but also on his quickness and agility. The quicker and more agile he is, the closer he can line up to the offensive blocker (1 yard). If he lacks quickness, then his alignment will be about 2 yards from the offensive blocker (Diagram 10-1), so that he never gets hooked by the end.

Three-Point Stance

Since the two-point stance is fairly common, its discussion will not be included here. However, in order for the defensive end to charge to his control point of responsibility, from where he will react to his key and the football, he should employ a three-point stance. It will be similar to that of the other linemen (Chapter 9) only more elongated, since he is permitted to have more weight forward on his down hand and an increase in the distance between his feet of about 1 foot. Since the end is charging on a pre-determined course, he should be turned in at about a 45° angle with the line-of-scrimmage.

Key and Charge

Both ends should align with their *inside* foot back and *inside* hand down. Starting with the *inside* foot first, the end takes three quick steps into the offensive backfield, using the near back's outside hip (or where he would line up) as a key or as an aiming point. The end will offer only a hard surface of inside leg/inside arm to the blocker. This allows the end to force the play back inside, and by keeping the outside foot free, the end is able to maintain proper leverage for containment.

Diagram 10-1 illustrates the approximate alignment and charge of the defensive ends, as described above.

Diagram 10-1
Defensive ends charge to control point—react.

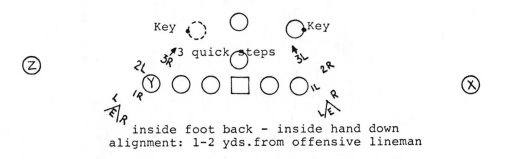

REACTIONS OF THE DEFENSIVE END

It is important for the defensive end to reach this prescribed point in a low stance and maintain control of this area, because he is trying to stop the play before it starts. His key will dictate his reactions.

If Key Goes Away from the End

If the defensive end's key goes away from him, the end should immediately look for the football coming back his way on a counter-play of some type (Diagram 10-2, left illustration). Should this occur, the defensive end must play off the lead blocker in the prescribed manner and keep the ball carrier contained.

If both the key and the football go away from the defensive end, he trails or chases at the depth of the football until it crosses the line-of-scrimmage, in the event the ball carrier or quarterback is forced to pull up as the result of not being able to get outside (Diagram 10-2,

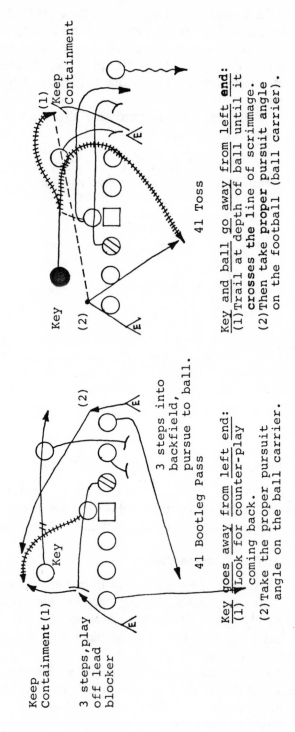

Diagram 10-2

Reaction of (left) end when key goes away from his position.

right illustration). When the football crosses the line-of-scrimmage, the defensive end takes a pursuit angle on the ball carrier in order to cut off the latter should he break back against the grain of the play. He should not continue to chase the play from behind. (The importance of proper pursuit and numerous coaching points were discussed in Chapter 9.) In the defensive scheme if another defender is assigned as trail or chase man, the defensive end takes his pursuit angle on the ball carrier immediately after charging to his point of responsibility.

If Key Comes Toward the End

If his key comes toward the defensive end, the offensive back is either going to try: (A) to hook or overblock; (B) block out; (C) run at the end and/or release in the flat; (D) dive (or fake dive) inside; (E) set up in pocket protection (Diagram 10-3).

Diagram 10-3
Reaction of (left) end when key comes toward his position.

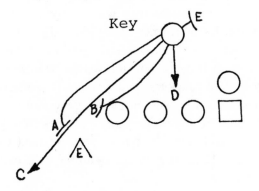

If the key (split back) attempts (A) or (B), the defender fights pressure, keeping the play contained inside, and he does not permit the ball carrier to get outside of his position.

If the key releases at the end but does not block him (C), the defender looks for the belly play, or the belly fake, and for the quarterback to retain the football on the option. If the key (split back) dives inside (D), the defensive end also looks for the quarterback to keep the football on the option. Should the latter occur in (C) and/or (D), then the defensive end applies his technique and the option responsibility which has been assigned to him. When his key sets up for pocket pass protection (E), the reaction and pass rush techniques for the end will be discussed in Chapter 11.

Do Not Lose Containment. If the key sets up in pocket protection (E), then the end must read pass, screen or draw. He must keep leverage on the passer and always know who has containment. Pursuit is practically worthless if containment is lost or breaks down. It is important to know whether it is *rush and contain, contain and rush* or *contain.* The scouting report and study of the game films will indicate how the defensive ends will play on their pass rush. Several illustrations will clarify these points.

Does the quarterback (passer) want to run with the football? Does he want to throw the ball? Is he a scrambler? Is he a runner? If the scouting report reveals the quarterback (passer) would rather run with the football, or if he is a better runner than a passer, then the ends (or whoever is assigned containment) must *contain* and *rush.* If the quarterback does not want to run with the football or runs with it only as a last resort when his receivers are covered, or if he is a poor runner, then the contain defenders can *rush* and *contain.* They can afford to gamble and attempt to beat the blocker to the inside on occasion, since percentage-wise they will be correct more often than in the first situation. In the former illustration, they are more likely to be wrong than right percentage-wise, so they must contain and rush from the outside-in. A third illustration would be in *man* coverage for your secondary and linebackers, and *you must contain,* as your defenders who have secondary containment (generally linebackers) will be driven off in man coverage. Therefore, if the end (who has containment) goes to the inside and the passer gets outside, it will generally result in a long run. Therefore, in the defenses with *man* coverage, it is imperative to *contain.*

COACHING POINTS

The following coaching points are important for successful defensive end play:

1. Know your responsibility on every play.
2. Do your job first; help second.
3. Contain all plays—play ball at its depth in the backfield.
4. Use your hands, arms and shoulders to protect yourself. Keep the blocker away from your body and legs. Keep on balance and meet the blocker with your inside leg forward.

5. Stay low and play through the blocker's head. Pursue and tackle the ball carrier.

6. Always stay on your feet. Do not be knocked down—and never blocked out by one blocker! Stay squared off.

7. Be aggressive; make something happen. Have confidence, and do not be afraid of making a mistake. Get into the defensive backfield.

8. Give ground grudgingly. Hold all gains to 2 yards or less.

Additional coaching points for the defensive end are offered in Chapter 11.

SELECTED DRILLS REFERENCE**

(*See* footnote source for 35 drills for teaching defensive line fundamentals, skills and techniques.)

** Donald E. Fuoss, *Championship Football Drills for Teaching Offensive and Defensive Fundamentals and Techniques* (Englewood Cliffs, N.J.: Prentice-Hall, Inc., 1964), pp. 220-236.

INTRODUCTION

A team's pass defense will only be as good as the pressure the defensive line in particular puts on the passer. In present-day football, an aggressive pass rush is mandatory. The best pass defense is a tough rush, and a successful rush does not mean only trapping the passer behind the line-of-scrimmage. A pass rush is highly effective if, in addition to tackling the passer on occasion, you force him to scramble and throw poorly or destroy his timing so that he throws incompletions or interceptions.

Rushing the passer with only a four- or five-man front has become an exacting science in recent years. Previously linemen were merely instructed to "Rush the passer," but very little time was spent in teaching the defenders *how* to do the job! Pass protection techniques (Chapter 8) have become so sophisticated that you can no longer rely on the "dogs" and blitzes alone to get to the passer. Then, too, offensive-minded coaches have just about reduced the defensive alignment to a four-man rush, so that it is imperative the pass rush techniques be effective or the offense will pick the defense apart with a short, effective passing game.

PASS RUSH PRINCIPLES AND COACHING POINTS

Approximately a dozen pass rush principles, with accompanying coaching points, will be discussed

11

Coaching Pass Rush Fundamentals, Skills and Techniques

first. Therefore, both coach and player will understand what the defensive player must try to accomplish in order to be an effective pass rusher.

Recognize and Identify "Pass"

The defensive linemen, as well as the defensive secondary and linebackers, should recognize and identify "Pass." Linemen must be taught to read the difference when an offensive blocker sets up to pass block or draw block, and when he sets up to "influence" a defender —and, identify each principle correctly: "Pass," "Draw," "Trap," "Screen," etc.

Close Rushing Distance Quickly

Quickness is probably the most important single factor in successfully rushing the passer. Strength and toughness are important, but the defender must get the jump on the blocker and literally *sprint* or *explode* into his man. The defender cannot reach for the blocker, as he must close the rushing distance quickly and engage his man, hands high on the pads, helmet or chest, feet up under his own body. The rusher must beat the blocker first. To aid the rusher in getting to the blocker quickly, he should get as close as possible to the football or the line-of-scrimmage.

Stay in the Rushing Lane

The rusher must always move *toward* the passer. Therefore, he must adjust to the flow of the football, whether it is a straight dropback pass, a play action pass, semi- or sprint-out pass, bootleg or waggle pass, etc., and regardless of whether it is to or away from his side of the line-of-scrimmage. In each instance he approaches the passer from a different angle or position, and he must be drilled versus each of these situations. Then, too, he is in the running defense first, and in the pass defense (as a pass rusher) secondly. In every situation, however, the pass rusher must stay in his rushing lane, or he will leave a void in the defensive front and pursuit pattern. When he makes his move to go by his offensive blocker, he must do so quickly and close immediately to his rushing lane.

Get Under Blocker's Pads and Keep Feet Moving

What the rusher is trying to do is get to the blocker as quickly as possible, start turning him one way and then rush the passer the other way. The defender must try to turn the blocker's shoulders *perpendicular* to the line-of-scrimmage, while the rusher wants to keep his own shoulders *parallel* to the line-of-scrimmage. The rusher must take short, choppy steps, have "quick feet," turn the blocker, step by him and stay in his rushing lane.

Release from the Blocker

Once the rusher engages the blocker, he should try to get by him as quickly as possible. The defender should *not* continue to push and shove the blocker, but as soon as he recognizes and identifies "Pass," the rusher should disengage from the blocker as quickly as possible. However, he must stay in his rushing lane as he disengages his blocker, and always move directly toward the passer. Therefore, the rusher should release as close as possible to his blocker and take the most direct route in getting to the passer.

Never Be Driven by the Passer (Ball)

A blocker will generally invite his man to the outside, and he will block the rusher immediately if he attempts to take the inside path to the football. Conversely, in rushing from the outside (generally a defensive end), the rusher should not permit the blocker to "wheel" him beyond the passer or the ball. Therefore, as the rusher approaches a point in his charge of approximately a yard from the passer or ball, and his blocker has an inside position on the rusher and is still taking the latter to the outside, the rusher might have to move quickly to the inside or he will be driven beyond the passer and the football. Should the latter occur, the rusher is ineffective in his rushing tactics, and if he is an end, the passer now has the choice either of stepping up into the pocket to throw or getting outside of containment, since the rusher has been driven beyond the football. Mention was made in Chapter 10 as to the importance of proper containment.

Do Not Jump at the Passer; Get Hands High

Two glaring errors in rushing the passer are for the rusher to raise his hands upward when he is *not* near the passer, and jumping in the air in an effort to block the pass when the passer pumps the ball.

At times rushers are still engaged at the line-of-scrimmage but will have their hands up in the air, making excellent blocking surfaces for the blockers. The rusher should use his arms to aid him in his running in getting to the passer quickly, and not attempt to run with his arms raised in the air in getting to the passer until the latter starts to release the football to a receiver. Then the hands should go "up high"!

When Facing the Passer. When the rusher is facing the passer, he should not jump into the air or leave his feet in the pass rush. At times the passer will check his throw, duck under the leaping rusher and then either run or pass successfully.

When Rushing from the Blind Side. If the rusher is coming from the blind side he can hurdle a blocker, and he can lunge at the passer in an effort to "undress him" from the ears down. The rusher from the blind side goes for the passer's arm and the football, attempting to knock the ball loose before the latter starts his forward passing motion. However, he, too, tackles the passer high, coming from the top down on him.

Tackle from the Top Down; "Undress" the Passer

The rusher should come in on the passer *high* for several reasons:

1. By raising his hands just as the passer attempts to release the football, the latter must release the ball at a higher angle which leads to interceptions or incompletions. When tackling him low, this permits the passer to drill the football to a receiver despite the fact that a rusher might be around his waist.

2. By tackling from the top down there is a possibility of deflecting the football, or of knocking the ball loose for a fumble if the passer does not release the football.

3. High tackling is more punishing to the passer than to tackle him lower, as both of the rusher's arms crash down over the passer's head and body and the rusher drives into the passer, headgear-to-headgear.

Yell "Ball" on Release; Break on Throw

All rushers yell "Ball" to alert their teammates the football is in the air, to get all defenders to break on the throw and to change from defense to offense.

A rusher may still be engaged with his blocker, or a rusher might be on the ground, but when he hears "Ball," he knows the football is now on the defensive side of the line-of-scrimmage, and he should attempt to locate the football and get to it immediately. His objective now is to make the tackle and try to knock the receiver loose from the football.

Knock the Receiver Loose from the Football

Many times it is a defensive lineman coming back into the defensive secondary who knocks the ball loose from the receiver. The receiver observes the secondary defenders and linebackers in the immediate area where he catches the football. He has a chance to brace himself as he is about to be tackled or as he attempts to evade these defenders. Generally, he is not set for the tackle from behind or the blind side. Frequently this knocks the ball loose from the receiver, or vice versa if the tackle is vicious enough. Therefore, a coach should drill his rushers to peel back, hustle upfield and get in on the tackle before the play is whistled dead.

Do Not Lose Morale Because of Completions

There is no defense against the perfectly thrown pass, although its completion is discouraging. Secondly, there will probably be a number of completions, but one interception will nullify a number of them, providing the offense does not score often on the passes which are completed. If you get two interceptions out of every 14 attempted, you will generally have a successful pass defense. Defensive morale means maintaining confidence and not panicking when the opposition completes several passes. The next pass will be the interception!

Always Know Who Has Containment; Never Lose It

The importance of always knowing who has containment and cognizance of whether it is *rush* and *contain, contain* and *rush* or *contain,* was discussed previously (Chapter 10).

PASS RUSH TECHNIQUES AND COACHING POINTS

There are a large number of different pass rush techniques which may be used, but it would be best to perfect only several. Time is always of the essence in coaching. To try to master a number of different techniques in order to accomplish the same objective frequently, means the player does not become competent in any of them and fails to perform effectively.

Simply stated, the rusher must start the blocker turning one way, and generally he then rushes the other way. Exceptions will be noted. The defender must try to turn the blocker's shoulders perpendicular to the line-of-scrimmage, while the rusher wants to keep his shoulders parallel to the line-of-scrimmage. He attempts to "break the square" of the blocker's position.

All the pass rusher's techniques begin by engaging the blocker, with hands high on his pads, chest or helmet. If there is a physical mismatch, the defender drives the blocker into the passer.

A proficient pass rusher will make his various movements all in one fluid move.

Butt and Reach or Butt, Grab and Turn Techniques

The pass rusher hitting on the rise drives the top of his headgear up under the chin of the blocker, "popping" his opponent's head back. He should not over-extend his body. He should keep his feet moving and square off with the blocker, so that the rusher is lined up with him in the middle of his body. The rusher's hands should come up quickly and grab the rear portion of the blocker's shoulder pads. The rusher pulls the blocker's left shoulder with his right hand, and quickly reaches over the blocker's left shoulder with his left hand. The rusher must step around the blocker's left side quickly, and then adhere to the pass rush principles mentioned above.

The procedure would be reversed if the rusher were going by the blocker's right side to get to the passer.

The pass rusher must "reach" over the pass blocker's shoulder quickly and get by his opponent with speed or he will present a good blocking surface to the blocker.

Pull and Push (or Push and Pull) Techniques

A variation of the above technique is to square off with the blocker the same as above, only pull with the right hand from the rear of the blocker's left shoulder and push with the left hand on the blocker's right shoulder, going around the blocker's left side to get to the passer.

The procedure would be reversed if the rusher were going around the blocker's right side.

The opposite of the pull and push technique is to push first and pull second. The rusher squares off with the blocker and slams him high on the front of the left shoulder with his right hand, and with his left hand pulls the blocker's right elbow in an arm-drag technique, stepping around the blocker's right side; i.e., the side he is pulling on.

Grab and Turn Techniques

These represent a variation of a couple of techniques, starting with the one explained first where the rusher grabs the blocker by his shoulder pads. The rusher starts like he is going to turn the blocker to the rusher's right. The blocker will generally shift his weight in that direction to fight pressure. The rusher now drives back to his left quickly, going by the blocker on his right side to get to the passer. In getting back to his left side, the rusher may have to use a "reach" technique or a pull or arm-drag technique, if he does not turn the blocker sufficiently in his initial "grab" technique. Either a push and pull or pull and push technique would accomplish the same objective.

Drive-By or Change-Up Techniques

A drive-by technique by a defensive end who is being blocked by an offensive back is a good change-up, especially if the rusher has been going inside on occasion when another defender had containment.

The defensive end, coming from the outside, has a chance to see the offensive back set up to pass block, and the latter has a chance to observe the defender coming on his rush. The rusher should *look* at the *inside* hip of the blocker, like he is concentrating on trying to beat his man to the inside. At the last second, as he approaches the offensive back who is assigned to block the defensive end, the latter should close on the blocker, head fake at the inside hip of his man and drive by him quickly to the outside.

Club and Helmet Slap Techniques

While the professional football players use the "club" and helmet slap techniques quite effectively, in high school and college football the employment of such methods might draw penalties; therefore, they will not be included here.

Practice Hurdling Blockers

Many blockers will try to cut down the pass rushers, generally when they are about to lose their men, by throwing at the knees-shins of the defenders. If rushers have not practiced against this method, they will be stymied at the line-of-scrimmage and their pass rushing will be ineffective. Therefore, in a coach's pass rush drills he must practice against this method, as rushers must be taught to hurl blockers who try to cut them down by throwing at their knees.

SELECTED DRILLS REFERENCE*

(*See* footnote source for 35 drills for teaching defensive line fundamentals, skills and techniques.)

* Donald E. Fuoss, *Championship Football Drills for Teaching Offensive and Defensive Fundamentals and Techniques* (Englewood Cliffs, N.J.: Prentice-Hall, Inc., 1964), pp. 220-236.

INTRODUCTION

The real heart of any defense is good linebacking. There never has been a strong defensive team with incapable linebackers. A team must have good linebacking in order to have a strong defense. A linebacker who is not sound fundamentally will make any kind of defensive line look weak, and outstanding linebacking can strengthen a mediocre line. In building a defensive unit, therefore, prime consideration must be given to the selection of good athletes for the linebacking positions. After that it becomes a matter of coaching.

LINEBACKING PERSONNEL

Your linebackers are your *"search and destroy men."* They need a rare combination of ability. They need physical size in order to stand tough against the run, and they need speed to cover offensive backs on man coverage coming out of the backfield. Linebackers need physical toughness and tremendous agility in order to have instantaneous reactions.

Football Sense or Smartness

Your linebackers must have good football sense or smartness. Through repetitive drill, most players can be taught play recognition and offensive tendencies. Comprehension of this information is important in order to attain maximum results in defensing the opposition's

12

Coaching Linebacker Fundamentals, Skills and Techniques

offense. Linebackers should have the ability to diagnose the opposition's plays quickly and surely, and then react immediately to the play.

On every play, a linebacker must be cognizant of what the opposition must accomplish or gain in order to maintain possession of the football. This is probably the most important single factor for technically sound defensive football.

Linebackers Must Be Masters of Proper Pursuit Angles. The good linebackers know the correct angles of pursuit versus every play. This is another facet of football smartness. By studying the offensive attack and its personnel, the linebacker can judge his speed in relation to the ball carrier's. After the primary line of defense makes its commitment, the linebacker is usually in the best position to make the tackle, which should be near the line-of-scrimmage in the normal situation. If the ball carrier should get by the linebacker, the latter must change his course and attempt to intercept the runner by using the proper angle of pursuit in a second effort to tackle him.

Keep Leverage on the Ball Carrier. Misjudging the speed of the ball carrier is a common mistake that places the linebacker at a disadvantage. If he over-runs the play, he cannot maintain the proper leverage on the ball carrier, who will now be in a position to cut back through the linebacker's vacated territory. Over-running the play also permits blockers to knock the linebacker beyond the running lane, preventing him from maintaining proper leverage on the ball carrier. By employing the proper pursuit angle, the linebacker can use his teammates or the sideline as an ally.

Must Have a "Nose" for the Football

All of his attributes are of little importance and significance if the linebacker lacks the courage or desire to make the tackle. All of his efforts will have been for naught if he misses the tackle. Consequently, the linebacker must be a good tackler (Chapter 13).

LINEBACKER'S STANCE

It is important for the linebacker to take the proper stance and make the correct alignment, so he can come into an effective *hitting position* and react properly when the play begins. While his stance and individual alignment will depend mostly upon the defense and the tactical situation, fundamentally a good football stance for the linebacker is as follows:

1. Semi-upright, two-point stance, with the weight equally distributed on the balls of the feet, approximately shoulder width, toes pointed straight ahead, feet parallel and either even or slightly staggered. If the latter position, the inside foot should be in advance of the outside foot in a toe-to-instep or heel relationship, depending upon which feels the most comfortable to the linebacker.

   The positioning of the feet depends on the individual coach, and what he wants the linebacker to accomplish. As an illustration, with the feet even and parallel, the linebacker can move laterally in either direction more quickly. With the feet staggered and parallel, the linebacker cannot move as quickly laterally to his inside as to his outside, since the inside foot is forward. In this position, however, the linebacker can move back to his hook zone, laterally to his outside or forward, to meet an offensive blocker more quickly. Regardless of the foot position, it is imperative for the linebacker to meet the blocker, firing out at him with the inside foot forward.

2. The knees are flexed slightly and point straight ahead.

3. The hips are flexed and the body crouched slightly, in a comfortable position.

4. The shoulders should be parallel with the line-of-scrimmage, and the arms should hang straight down with a slight bend at the elbows. The hands are generally slightly clenched. The hands or elbows should *not* be placed on the knees or thighs.

5. The head and eyes should be in such a position as to allow the linebacker to see his key. His stance should be such that his line of vision will be nearly parallel to the ground as he watches his key, reacting immediately to it and the football.

In spite of all of the techniques for the Oklahoma 5-2, 4-3, 4-4 et al, linebackers are not the same; many of the coaching points, defensive principles and fundamentals are applicable to the linebacker's position regardless of alignment.

Alignment

It is imperative for the linebacker to take his correct lateral and vertical alignment, which will depend on the defensive alignment being employed (Diagram 12-1, Oklahoma 5-2 illustrated). Fundamentally, the linebacker's vertical position will be approximately 1½–2 yards off the line-of-scrimmage in a *normal* situation—although his depth depends on how deep he can play and still hold his ground, and how tight he can play and still support at the corner, and get back on passes. The tactical situation is always a determining factor and can never be discounted. In a short-yardage situation, excluding the other tactical factors, the linebacker normally will move closer to the line-of-scrimmage. Conversely, on long yardage the linebacker normally will loosen so interior linemen cannot legally fire out and block him on a pass play. He is also closer to covering his pass responsibility. The Oklahoma 5-2 linebacker's lateral alignment will be off-set and his inside ear aligned to the guard's outside ear.

REACTION TECHNIQUES

As part of the forcing unit of the defense, the linebacker must be able to handle the running play to his area first. If the run does not hit in his area, then he must free himself and move to the ball. He should stop inside plays and pursue the wide plays from inside-out. He must move at an angle which will put him in front of the ball carrier at the earliest possible moment.

In Diagram 12-1 (center illustration) the Oklahoma 5-2 linebacker keys through his guard to his near back, and can expect the four possibilities listed below when the (right) guard does the following:

(A) Blocks *in* on the *nose-man* (middle guard)—expect the *trap* (Diagram 4-1, 28 Trap), (Diagram 4-5, right illustration, 30 Trap), (Diagram 6-7, 40 Trap), with the *tackle blocking down;* or the *blast* (Diagram 4-1, 28 Blast), with the offensive *backs leading through* on isolation.

(B) Blocks inside-*out* on linebacker—except on an inside running play up-the-middle, such as a drive, pick, sneak, buck (Diagram 6-8, 39 Buck).

(C) Steps for outside position on (*hook blocks*) *linebacker*—expect an *outside* play (Diagram 6-12, 42 Flip), (Diagram 6-14, 24 Power), (Diagram 9-2, right illustration, 42 Toss), et al.

(D) Blocks *out* on *tackle*—look for the offensive tackle pulling behind and blocking through, and a delayed running play up-the-middle.

(*See* footnote reference for a detailed discussion of reaction techniques.*)

---

* Donald E. Fuoss, "Techniques of Linebacking," *Summer Manual,* American Football Coaches Association, June 1963, pp. 47-54.

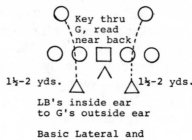

Basic Lateral and
Vertical Alignment

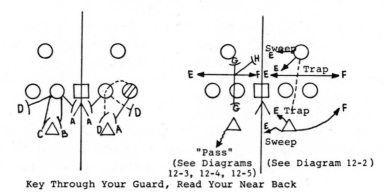

Key Through Your Guard, Read Your Near Back

Diagram 12-1
Key and reactions of Oklahoma 5-2 linebackers.

Leverage Principles and "Hitting" Techniques

Regardless of the defensive alignment, the linebacker should react as follows and adhere to the following leverage principles and techniques, versus a lineman blocking out on him, Diagram 12-1, (B)-(C) illustrations:

1. Continue to maintain the proper (ear-to-ear) alignment (Oklahoma 5-2), sliding very quickly with a short, lateral step if necessary. Move the outside foot first in order to maintain proper alignment if blocker steps for *outside* position (C). A common error is for the linebacker to jab step forward when the blocker is stepping for position on him. Maintaining proper alignment and not being caught out of position will always put the linebacker in a good position to deliver a blow to the blocker. The purpose of which is to keep leverage on the blocker, and which will destroy his block, control him and not permit him to get to the linebacker's vulnerable area.

2. Jab step with the inside foot at the head of the blocker, maintaining the *hitting* position throughout. The linebacker should not step back when the blocker fires out at him or comes to the side of him.

3. Deliver a blow to the blocker's chest with a forearm lift, the purpose of which is to raise him and destroy his block so that the linebacker can continue to move with the ball and not be tied up by the blocker. The technique of delivering the blow from underneath the opponent is for the linebacker to jab step, dip his tail, get his shoulder up under the head of the blocker and slam the forearm into the chest.

4. Shed the blocker and fight pressure. The opposite hand is placed against the blocker's helmet, and the linebacker can shed him by pushing against the head. This is especially true if the blocker has gotten through the linebacker's block protection and the latter has lost his leverage on the blocker. If he has executed the fundamentals properly and has maintained leverage on the blocker, simply by throwing out his hitting arm the linebacker can shed the blocker. It is a shoving action with the hitting arm to throw off the blocker, and a pushing action with the opposite hand. The linebacker cannot be driven in or out, and should never be knocked off his feet, opening an alley through which the ball carrier can run if the play is striking in the linebacker's immediate area. (*See* Chapter 3, Diagram 3-3, *Ward-Off and Shed Drill.*)

With the offensive lineman pulling (E) on-side, and (F) behind his center, respectively (Diagram 12-1, right illustration), the linebacker should immediately key his near back. Diagram 6-5 illustrates 34 Gee, with the tackle blocking down and the guard pulling on-side (E). (42 Sweep would also have the guard pulling behind and the tackle blocking down, Diagram 6-11.)

When moving laterally to pursue the ball carrier, especially from the off-side, the linebacker should bow back *slightly* in the direction of the play in order to clear the line blocking. The first step is with the foot to the side the linebacker is going. He should maintain eye contact with the ball and not over-run the play, as was explained previously.

By reading the near back when the guard pulls behind his center (F), the linebacker can read trap (39 or 49 Trap) or sweep action (41 Sweep). However, Diagram 12-2 illustrates the guards going opposite the flow of the backs, and the linebackers must read *bootleg* action (41 Bootleg Pass) and knock off the crossing (Y) receiver if possible.

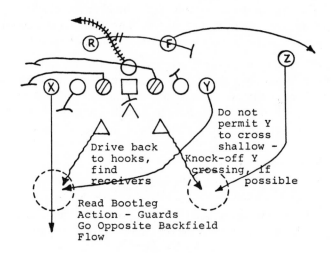

Drive back
to hooks,
find
receivers

Do not
permit Y
to cross
shallow -
Knock-off Y
crossing, if
possible

Read Bootleg
Action - Guards
Go Opposite Backfield
Flow

Diagram 12-2
Reaction of linebackers versus bootleg pass.

Reading "Pass" Action. In (G) and (H) the linebackers also read pass action, and react as indicated in Diagram 12-3 versus straight drop-back pass, Diagram 12-4 versus sprint-out pass and Diagram 12-5 versus play action pass. These will be explained because the principles and techniques are similar regardless of the defensive alignment. If the linebacker's key sets up in a block for a drop-back pass (Diagram 12-3), the linebacker should drop quickly to his hook zone (10 yards deep opposite the offensive end's normal position). His techniques are as follows: shout "Pass" as soon as he reads key properly; shift his attention to the quarterback and get to his hook zone; through peripheral vision, check the end to his side as he retreats. He will cover his hook area first, but slides to the flat if his area is void and/or the receiver has gone into the flat. The linebacker might also have side screen responsibility.

Techniques for Getting to the Hook Zone and Covering the Receiver. There is a difference of opinion among coaches as to the *best* technique for the linebacker to use in getting back to his hook zone and covering the receiver on the drop-back pass. Many coaches advocate teaching a drop-step, cross-over, sprint-back technique as soon as the linebacker reads "Pass." After his second cross-over step, the linebacker takes one more step, turns squaring off and continues to back up with short steps as he faces the passer, body under control, ready to react right, left or jump to intercept the ball, in the event the passer tries to throw the pass over his head.

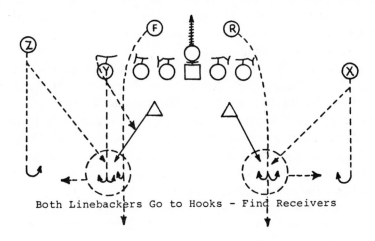

Diagram 12-3
Reaction of linebackers versus drop-back pass.

Since the passer is not going to throw the football to the defender, the latter must move either: (1) to play the ball through the receiver or (2) play the anticipated flight by reacting to the passer's first throwing motion. If he waits until the football leaves the passer's hand, he will not be able to get in front of the ball to intercept it or deflect it if the pass is thrown accurately.

At times a good passer will fake the throw first, pumping the ball, then throw after the linebacker has reacted to his initial arm movement. Nevertheless, the linebacker, unless playing the ball through the receiver or covering him so closely that the passer will not attempt to throw to this player, must get in position to play the passer's first arm motion. He tries to force the passer to throw over or through him. It *appears* that fewer passes are completed when the linebacker covers the receiver tightly, rather than positioning himself to play the first throwing motion of the passer. By the same measure, since he is concentrating on *looking up* the receiver in order to play him tightly or play the ball through him, it *appears* there are fewer interceptions by the linebacker when employing this technique. Conversely, the opposite *appears* to be the case, relevant to completions and interceptions, when the linebacker employs the drop-back technique. These are merely observations with which all coaches are not likely to agree, since there is a definite difference of opinion as to the *best* technique; i.e., play the anticipated flight of the ball or look up the receiver and cover him closely.

Techniques Versus the Action Pass and the Sprint-Out Pass. Versus the sprint-out pass (Diagram 12-4) the linebackers play for the pass first, since the quarterback is sprinting out at an angle *away* from the line-of-scrimmage and there is *no running action threat.* [Note backfield action is similar but *different* versus the Tailback Draw or Delay (Diagram 8-20, front side; Diagram 8-21, back side) and the Fake Tailback Draw Pass (Diagram 8-14, front side only).] Versus the play action pass (Diagram 12-5), the on-side linebacker may be drawn in by a good faking action in the backfield. Should this occur, the on-side linebacker should continue to rush the passer (or tackle the faking back) since it will be difficult to drop off into the flat, and impossible to get back to the hook zone.

Assuming the fake is poor, however, and the on-side linebacker reads *pass,* he would play both the sprint-out and play action passes the same then, attempting to drive back to his hook area and look up a receiver. If he is "late" in reading *pass* in that a good fake holds him at the line-of-scrimmage, but he does not make the tackle and he is not caught in the line, he may continue to the flat zone attempting to look up a receiver in that area. Should the defensive end lose containment and the quarterback challenges the corner with the football, the on-side linebacker has secondary containment responsibilities (Diagrams 12-4 and 12-5)

The off-side linebacker, if properly trained, will read all three passing actions the same (Diagrams 12-3, 12-4 and 12-5), reading his key's back-side protection technique as *pass,* and he will open to the outside and look up a receiver coming into his area. While he might mis-read the play action pass (Diagram 12-5), he should never mis-read the quarterback's sprint-out action (Diagram 12-4). Should he mis-read his key, and then recognize pass, he should either attempt to drive back into the middle and look up a crossing receiver or go to the on-side linebacker's hook spot. Both linebackers' pass responsibility will be coordinated with the secondary defenders'.

LINEBACKER'S STUNTING GAME TECHNIQUES**

For the linebacker to be successful in directing the defense, there must be a systemized and simple method of stunting. While there are a number of individual and team stunts which may be employed (Dia-

---

** *Ibid.*
Also *see* Donald E. Fuoss, "Purdue's Coordinated Defensive Line Play Techniques and Stunts," *Summer Manual,* American Football Coaches Association, June 1967, pp. 33-40.

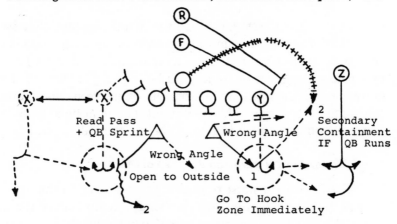

Both Linebackers Go to Hooks - Find Receivers

Diagram 12-4

Reaction of linebackers versus sprint-out pass.

Diagram 12-5

Reaction of linebackers versus action pass.

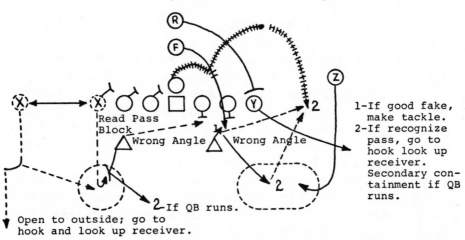

grams 8-1 to 8-5, as illustrations), regardless of the ones used the linebacker cannot be indecisive. Should this occur he is generally caught in the line, and is ineffective either as a rusher or defender and is unable to pursue properly. The linebacker will also want to conceal his intention of stunting. At other times he should fake or "dummy" a stunt, attempting to confuse the offensive linemen in their blocking patterns.

Should he have to alter his alignment or stance noticeably in order to get to his area of responsibility on his stunt, he should do so quickly and at the last second, so the offensive players cannot adjust their blocking patterns and block the defensive stunt effectively. The latter is apt to occur if he moves too soon or the snap count is delayed, and the football is not put into play immediately after he has revealed by his new alignment or stance that he is going to stunt. Yet when he moves he will draw attention from the offensive linemen, and by observing their reactions to his movements he might be able to determine where the offensive play is directed before the ball is put into play.

Understand Nature and Purpose of Stunts

The linebacker must thoroughly understand the nature and purpose of the stunts. Is it a stunt involving only his side of the defensive line and the other side operates independently? Is it a coordinated team stunt? When is the stunt *on; off?* If the stunt is *on,* the linebacker may go through with it regardless of the action in the backfield. He makes an all-out effort to penetrate the line or draw a block in order to free a teammate to get into the offensive backfield. Or the linebacker's key, generally a back and/or the ball, will indicate whether the stunt is *on* or *off.*

Scrape-Off and Shuffle Techniques. In Diagram 9-2 the interior linemen slant/loop to their right, with the defender over the offensive right end using an anchor technique. Although the left linebacker's key may be a back, should the offensive right guard block out on him, he must fill the hole. He must stop the plays where the guard blocks out. These techniques were explained previously. If the ball goes to the pocket the stunt is *off,* and both linebackers go to their respective hook zones. If the flow of the play comes toward the left linebacker (Diagram 9-2, right illustration), since his teammate is employing an anchor technique on the offensive end and his defensive tackle is slanting to his right to handle traps and counters, versus a running play or an action pass to his side, he scrapes off behind his tackle, firing into the off-tackle hole; i.e., the stunt is *on.* If the flow is away from him, the stunt is *off.* If he recognizes an action pass as the flow goes away, his course will either be deep middle or taking his teammate's hook zone to his right. Both techniques were discussed previously.

The right linebacker reacts as follows as he keys the left halfback: If pocket pass, go to hook zone (stunt is *off*). If flow is away, off-side linebacker may or may not have option of filling hard to ball, probably between offensive right guard-center gap versus running play (*on*); versus action pass away, he either shuffles back getting depth in middle or covers teammate's hook zone, using the techniques described previously. Then the stunt is *off*. Should the near back dive, the right linebacker fills the hole between the offensive left guard and tackle (*on*). Should the flow of the play come toward the right linebacker (Diagram 9-2, left side), he may run through (as above) or he plays football out of the line; i.e., pursue inside-out. Since the defensive line is slanting/looping to their right, should the offensive left guard pull or attempt to block the linebacker, the middle guard is free. If the offensive left tackle blocks down on the linebacker, the defensive right tackle should be free. The linebacker is responsible for stopping counter-plays, with the near back leading. Therefore, if the halfback dives and flow goes away, the right (shuffle) linebacker must play his key and fill the hole.

If the slant of the defensive line were to the left and the linebackers were keying the offensive right halfback, the scrape-off and shuffle techniques would be reversed for the linebackers.

If a team was employing pattern defenses, depending upon offensive tendencies and the factors mentioned previously, the aforementioned might well be coordinated stunts, so that the linebackers' options would be eliminated and they would fire regardless. In Diagram 9-2 (right illustration) the line is slanting to the right, and the linebackers are firing in behind them to the left going through gaps.

Individual Defensive Stunts. Individual stunts may involve only one linebacker and one defensive lineman or half of the defensive line. Since cross-charges between a lineman and his linebacker are fairly common, individual stunts will not be discussed further. The tactical situation and offensive tendencies always dictate when a stunt should be employed, and which ones are likely to be the most effective. Even though the stunts are individual in nature, the entire defense must be coordinated in order to be sound defensively.

COACHING POINTS FOR LINEBACKERS

Additional coaching points for linebackers are as follows:

1. In a definite passing situation, loosen up, unless assigned to hold up an offensive end. In an obvious passing situation, look for a screen pass or the draw play. Some teams like to run a trap play up-the-middle in this situation.

2. When playing over an end, never allow him to release unmolested for a pass. Throw off the timing of the pass by pushing and shoving the receiver, forcing him to alter his pass route or direction. You cannot continue to "chug" the receiver if the latter breaks

beyond the linebacker, so that you must now turn your body and reach back in order to shove the eligible receiver.

3. Offensive linemen generally tip a drop-back pass by showing passive blocking or a retreating type of block protection immediately. The linebacker should yell "Pass" when he is convinced it is a pass and assume pass responsibility. While the linebacker generally is not responsible for the draw play, if the quarterback goes back as if to pass but hands off to another back, the linebacker should yell "Draw" and move in to tackle the ball carrier.

4. When a pass is thrown, break for and play the football. Be aggressive on pass defense, as the football belongs to whoever can catch it. The linebacker should attempt to get in front of the ball before it is released from the passer's hand. This forces the passer either to throw over the linebacker, attempt to drill the ball by him or alter his throw.

5. On an interception yell "Block" (or some other significant word), passing it down the line. If the linebacker is nearest the man for whom the pass was intended, he should block back on him. Otherwise he hustles to get in front of his teammate who has caught the pass, throwing at the first opponent who threatens the runback of the interception.

6. After penetrating across the line-of-scrimmage versus a well-executed action pass fake, which then develops into a pass, continue to rush the passer and force the play. It is almost impossible to recover quickly enough to be effective downfield as a pass defender under such circumstances.

7. When firing or *dogging,* do so on the snap of the ball. Then play as a lineman after penetrating the line-of-scrimmage, sliding with the running play and accelerating your rush if a pass develops.

8. When the territory between the tackle and end is the linebacker's responsibility and the block of the offensive end indicates an off-tackle play, the linebacker should guard against penetrating too deeply into the hole and getting trapped by the interference, thus widening the hole. Assuming he is not stunting or firing, if the linebacker meets the play in the hole and makes the tackle, he will have done his job effectively.

9. On running plays to the opposite side or when the flow is away, the off-side linebacker should look for the ball carrier cutting back inside of the on-side linebacker, or for the delayed receiver cutting across for the pass. In the latter case the linebacker should attempt to knock off the intended receiver, not permitting the latter to get behind him.

10. While there are additional coaching points for the linebacker, none is more important than the application of the defensive axiom: "Pursue, do not chase; angle, do not arc." His value to the defense always varies inversely with his distance from the football; therefore, the linebacker should know the proper "fill patter" of his teammates versus the opposition's running attack, in order to take the correct angle of pursuit on all plays.

SELECTED DRILLS REFERENCE***

(*See* footnote source for 28 football drills for teaching linebacking fundamentals, skills and techniques.)

*** Donald E. Fuoss, *Championship Football Drills for Teaching Offensive and Defensive Fundamentals and Techniques* (Englewood Cliffs, N.J.: Prentice-Hall, Inc., 1964), pp. 252-265.

Coaches differ in their opinion concerning the *best* tackling techniques, but all agree the objective is to down the ball carrier and/or prevent him from carrying out his specific assignment.

To execute all of the defensive fundamentals correctly preparatory to the actual tackle, and then fail to tackle or stop the ball carrier, *means total failure*. All has been in vain if the defensive players fail to accomplish this objective, since tackling is the ultimate of defensive football. On the other hand, *effective* tackling at times may consist of the defensive player hurling his body into the ball carrier, pushing an opponent into him, riding the ball carrier to the ground or grabbing his arm, foot, jersey or pant in order to stop him. These methods of tackling are not thought of as *picture* or *master* tackles where the tackler dominates and physically punishes the ball carrier, but they are effective if the ball carrier and his team do not reach their specific objective.

Regardless of the techniques employed, effective tackling is the ultimate of defensive football. From a defensive point-of-view, an offensive play is not complete until the ball carrier has been tackled or downed.

Basic Qualities: Desire and Form

Tackling consists of two basic qualities: *desire* or effort, and *form*

13

Coaching Tackling Fundamentals, Skills and Techniques

or ability. Of the two, desire is the most important requisite and generally is considered to be at least 75 per cent of effective tackling. If a player has the desire and "fire," generally he has the other inherent qualities of pride, morale and courage in order to tackle aggressively and effectively. It is a recognized fact that no coach can give a player who lacks "heart" these inherent qualities.

One's ability can be improved, since *form* can be taught and accounts for the remaining 25 per cent of tackling. A defensive man can usually bring down a ball carrier regardless of the form used if he has the determination and desire to get the job done. A player tackles better if he has the desire to dominate and master the ball carrier. In drilling, a coach should strive to teach his players the proper form in tackling, without destroying their desire and determination.

TACKLING PRINCIPLES AND COACHING POINTS

The *master tackle* is the ideal one for head-on tackling. It is the type of tackle that completely masters the ball carrier. It leaves little doubt in his mind as to who is the master of the situation. Despite the wide scope in techniques allowed a tackler, the following are the cardinal principles and fundamentals of good master tackling.

Get in a "Hitting" Position

The instant before contact as the tackler approaches the ball carrier, he should be in a *ready* or *hitting* position. This means having a good base, feet apart approximately shoulder width and moving with short, choppy steps, being careful not to over-stride, weight low in the tail and knees flexed in order to be able to uncoil and deliver a blow into the ball carrier. The back is relatively straight, head up, eyes on the football, which is the tackler's target, arms and hands away from the body in what is sometimes referred to as *gorilla* fashion, with body under control and on balance. From this good *hitting* position the tackler is able to shift with the runner, and his solid base gives him a good foundation for a driving tackle.

Drive Forehead Through the Football

The tackler must time his contact and drive his forehead through the football so as to get a good *shoulder* tackle. If the runner carries the football on either side of his body, the tackler's head will clear the ball carrier's body and he will get a solid shoulder tackle instead of an arm tackle. By directing his forehead rather than the top of his helmet at the football, the tackler can react better to the ball carrier since he is able to keep his eyes on the target. Very seldom does the good ball carrier run straight at an opponent or try to run over him, unless he has no other choice. Since the ball carrier is likely to fake one way and go another, the tackler must maintain a good base and not lose his target by lowering his head. He must have his head up and eyes open in order to see his target. There is no way of having power unless the tackler's head is up.

One of the objectives of defensive football is to gain possession of the football for the offense. A method of accomplishing this objective is to force the ball carrier to fumble the ball. By tackling in the prescribed manner, at times the tackler will butt the ball out of the ball carrier's arm, forcing him to fumble the football.

Take Away the Ball Carrier's Legs

As the tackler makes contact, he should extend the arms and hands and simultaneously *club* them around the ball carrier's body, employing a wrist lock or grasping his hands prior to using his strong back and leg muscles to lift the ball carrier off the ground. Depending on the respective size of the ball carrier and tackler, the latter might have to grab the ball carrier's buttocks or jersey if he is unable to grasp his own hands or use a wrist lock due to short arms. In any event, he should hit, hold on and lift by extending his body and legs, stopping the forward progress of the ball carrier, and take the latter's legs away from him. Many times a defensive man will make good shoulder contact but fail to make the tackle. The ball carrier's feet retain contact with the ground, he regains his balance and he continues running because the tackler fails to get his arm around the ball carrier and follow through.

Clubbing the arms does not mean swinging them open wide laterally, since the exaggerated arm swing usually causes the tackler to drop his head and/or stop. The tackler should not stop on contact, as he should *drive through the ball carrier*—not merely *to* him.

Do Not Permit the Ball Carrier to Fall Forward

The follow-through consists of hitting on the rise up into the ball carrier's numbers, picking him up and slamming him to the ground on his back or side with the tackler on top of him. The ball carrier should never be permitted to fall forward.

Apply Principles of Power and Leverage

Tackling relies heavily upon the application of the principles of power and leverage. Despite minor differences of opinion in the various techniques, good tackling is based upon these previously mentioned principles and fundamentals.

TACKLING TECHNIQUES AND COACHING POINTS

Head-on and angle or side tackling actually cover all classifications of tackling, although open-field, tackling from the rear and gang tackling techniques will be included, too.

Head-On Tackling Techniques

The head-on tackle generally is used in those situations in which the ball carrier has limited space in which to maneuver, and usually occurs at or near the line-of-scrimmage or in some cases in the close secondary. The tackler meets the ball carrier at the *cross-roads* and *chills* him. The fundamentals and techniques of head-on master tackling have been discussed already.

Angle or Side Tackling Techniques

Most of the tackles made in football are actually angle or side tackles, as seldom does a tackler meet the ball carrier head-on and execute a *picture* tackle. The fundamentals of the angle tackle were described previously for the master tackle, with the additional coaching point being the tackler places his head across and in front of the ball carrier. The objective is twofold: (1) it increases his tackling surface and gives additional power for the tackle; (2) in the event the tackler is not successful in making the tackle, but gets his head across and in front of the ball carrier, it forces the latter into pursuing tacklers. The objective is to keep containment on the ball carrier, turn him to the inside and keep him in front of the defenders. This will be discussed in greater detail shortly when considering team pursuit and gang tackling. Should the would-be tackler fail to turn the ball carrier to the inside, say as the result of incorrectly driving his head *behind* the runner, and he gets outside of containment, then the defenders become *chasers* instead of pursuers and it is merely a footrace between them and the ball carrier.

Some coaches still advocate teaching the cross-body roll technique on angle or side tackling, where the tackler hits with the shoulder, rolls across and turns underneath the ball carrier as he employs a downward twist of the body. Other coaches feel this takes away the results that are achieved through the master tackle, does not teach the rolling technique and lets the bodies fall as they will.

Pass Rush Tackling Techniques

Pass rush tackling techniques were discussed in Chapter 11.

Open-Field Tackling Techniques

Assuming the ball carrier gets beyond the line-of-scrimmage and is approaching the safety man or one of the defensive halfbacks, a good ball carrier has an advantage over the defender. The latter has too much territory to protect, and in such a situation the defender is not necessarily trying to save yards, but is trying to prevent a touchdown. Therefore, the defender must make the ball carrier commit himself to one side or the other, limiting his running room and the territory the defensive man must defend. When the ball carrier is in open field, he should be maneuvered to such a position that the tackler can run him out-of-bounds if he continues in the same line. If he cuts back, he will run into the arms of the tackler. This is a *sure* tackle, but it is not a *pretty* one, as the ball carrier must be tackled high (or pushed aggressively out-of-bounds). Many coaches do not advocate the *easy* method of pushing the player out-of-bounds, as this does not punish him physically, and few will permit their players to roll block the ball carrier, knocking him out-of-bounds.

If the ball carrier cannot be maneuvered into the sideline, the tackler must maneuver and retreat as he defends his goal line, until he can get help from his pursuing teammates. If the tackler must take his *shot* at the ball carrier, he must still force him to go only one way. He cannot permit the runner to have a two-way go. When they are even with each other then the tackler must go after the ball carrier aggressively, remembering to drive his head in front of the ball carrier, getting it between the runner and the goal line. It will be difficult for a slower defender to tackle a faster ball carrier once they are even with each other.

Tackling from the Rear Techniques

The same principles of tackling a player from the rear prevail as in the other types of tackles. Assuming a pursuing defender is overtaking a slower-running ball carrier, contact should be made about waist high, with the arms sliding downward to grasp the ball carrier's legs, dragging him to the ground. The tackler should aim high and be fairly close to the ball carrier before he dives for him, so that the latter's forward progress or his last-second evasive tactic does not carry him out of the tackler's range and grasp. The tackler should *not* leap on the ball carrier's back, as the latter is likely to carry him for extra yardage downfield.

Assuming the ball carrier is fast and is running away from the pursuer, any effort to tackle him generally is in desperation. One technique the tackler can use is to dive at the heels of the ball carrier, attempting to trip him by slapping the one (rear) foot hard toward his opposite foot. When the pursuer is successful, frequently this causes the ball carrier to trip and fall. Under such circumstances, the results may be considered more of "luck" than technique skillfully performed. The results are the same though.

Gang Tackling Techniques

The importance and necessity of the proper angles of team pursuit and gang tackling have been stressed several times already. The techniques of gang tackling have not been discussed.

There is a difference between gang tackling and piling on the ball carrier. There is also a difference between gang tackling where an effort is actually made to tackle the ball carrier, and the so-called questionable and controversial technique of *spearing* him with the headgear. The latter is not advocated, and should not be taught for numerous and obvious reasons.

Team Pursuit Defined. It is generally believed that the most important factor in defensive football today is the proper angle of team pursuit. Many coaches consider this as the starting point for a discussion on defensive football. *Team pursuit* may be defined as a planned system of converging upon the man who has the football as quickly as possible, with the idea of the entire defensive team operating as a flexible rubber band unit, containing the ball carrier inside of the defensive perimeter and maintaining proper pursuit angles in order to obtain gang tackling.

Gang tackling is the most demoralizing tactic in football, and is a *must* for good defensive play. It is the surest way of discouraging a ball carrier, who is *fair game* until the whistle blows halting the play or he is on the ground and cannot advance the football. Therefore, every defender should hustle to tackle the ball carrier on every play.

There have been many changes made in the game of football over the years. However, a team which displays desire, hustle and enthusiasm—each player working hard to improve his quickness, speed and tackling until he is doing his very best—will produce a squad that will win more than its share of football games.

SELECTED DRILLS REFERENCE*

(*See* footnote source for 26 drills for teaching tackling fundamentals, drills and techniques.)

---

* Donald E. Fuoss, *Championship Football Drills for Teaching Offensive and Defensive Fundamentals and Techniques* (Englewood Cliffs, N.J.: Prentice-Hall, Inc., 1964), pp. 272-284.